My
Kirkby
Childhood

by

Irene Birch
B.Ed (Hons)

© Irene Birch 1990

ISBN 0 903348 19 5

Print Origination (NW) Limited
Stephenson Way, Formby
Liverpool L37 8EG
07048 79231

Printed in Great Britain by
Billing & Sons Ltd, Worcester

Contents

PREFACE

Walking to school in the village of Kirkby, Lancashire, England, during 1939-46 was an unforgettable experience. As well as being exposed to the natural interests of country childhood, — collecting leaves and flowers to lovingly press inside thick books when we went home, or discovering another bird's nest which we hoped the 'townies' would not find, — our schooldays were also constantly being affected by the second world war, which had been instigated by Nazi Germany's invasion of Poland.

Imagine an older brother calling out, "Heh, look up there.", and, shifting our gaze, we looked upwards to the sky to see 2 planes apparently in combat — was it a 'dog fight'? We watched in awe, only to feel one's sleeve tugged as Donald reminded us that we would be late for school. He was exemplifying the attitude of our parents, and other British adults, that, no matter how hard the enemy tried to disrupt it, they were equally determined that our way of life would carry on as normally as possible.

PROLOGUE

I was prompted to write this account of my Kirkby childhood, by, firstly, the reaction of my former pupils at Ruffwood Comprehensive School. Whenever I mentioned 'old' Kirkby they always immediately showed interest and listened intently as I recounted a memory. From this I assumed they were keen to establish their own cultural background, history, and I have therefore written this contribution particularly for them, and for present and future generations of schoolchildren.

Secondly, it is in memory and honour of William Donald Birch, my belovèd brother who died on 30 June, 1987. During his brave, heroic fight against cancer we often talked of our childhood. Our shared memories brought Donald constant, lasting happiness and made me realise that if they were so important to him — a person of his stature and outstanding qualities — then they were worthy of being written down. They are here to express our mutual gratitude for, firstly, having such caring, hard-working, unselfish parents, — to us "the best in the world" (Don's words), and, secondly, for having had the good fortune to live in the village of Kirkby.

Croxteth Hall

1920: All tenants attend coming of age of Hugh, later 7th Earl of Sefton

Helena, 6th Countess of Sefton

Osbert, 6th Earl of Sefton

Lord and Lady Sefton's Wedding Day

Chapter I

Kirkby CE School and its surroundings
Lord Sefton

Sometimes when I go shopping to the Town Centre I don't hear the traffic and I don't see the crowds and the shops. Instead I hear a skylark as it soars high over quiet roads — a car being a rare sight. I see green fields with cattle grazing, wooded copses, the bluebell woods, hedgerows full of hawthorn blossom hiding birds' nests, and, ahead, the low-roofed sandstone building of Kirkby C of E Primary School. I particularly remember the Kirkby which existed 50 years ago between the years of 1939-1946, and I realise as I stand, for example, in Johnsons, the dry-cleaners, that I am in fact standing in the middle of one of Kirkby Hall farm's pastures.

Kirkby is now described as a "new town", as if Kirkby were created only 2 or 3 decades ago. It would perhaps be truer to state that a new town was built on the historic land known for centuries as the village of Kirkby, ie, Kirkby existed long before, centuries before, the idea of a new town was conceived. It has many connections with the history of our land, being part of the Nordic invasion of our shores, having an association with the conversion of Britons to Christianity, reflecting the feudal system practised in the middle ages — the land belonging to an earl, the village folk being his

Kirkby Hall Farm

tenants — and, not least of all, by playing a vital role in the defence of our nation during a world war.

The name "Kirk-by", meaning Church and Settlement, was conceived by the Vikings. In the Domesday Book, 1066, it appears as Cherchebi, held by Uctred. Its place in English history is also assured by the important part this then south-west Lancashire village, bounded by Simonswood, Knowsley, Fazakerley, and Melling, in the north west of England near Liverpool, played in helping to bring about world peace during the Second World War.

World War II started on my fifth birthday, 3 September 1939, the age at which I started school at Kirkby C of E Primary School, its only school. This was situated at the crossroads in the middle of Kirkby opposite the Village Hall *(its surrounding wall still remains, where the traffic lights are now, at the junction between County Road and Old Rough Lane).* The school was built of locally quarried sandstone. There were 2 playgrounds, one for the infants and one for the seniors. Games included, top and whip, hopscotch, marbles, conkers, shinty — *a kind of hockey,* and skipping — during one game of which we sang "On the mountain stands a lady . . . " and then invited a favourite friend, boy or girl, to join us in the rope as 2 others turned it. Boys were usually in short supply — probably too shy! Swimming lessons were not available.

Kirkby Parish Hall before extension

Entered from the infants playground a cloakroom led into Miss Cunningham's classroom where we learnt to read and write and to sing the rudiments of the music scale, she standing in front of a chart and pointing to each word as we tried to copy her tone — do, ray, me, etc. On the wall facing the class was a picture entitled "Faithful Unto Death" which expressed loyalty, an especially meaningful word in wartime Britain. It depicted a Roman centurion who remained at his post despite the volcano from Mount Vesuvius raging close by and its lava sweeping down to engulf the town of Pompeii in 79 AD *(The original of this painting by Sir Edward J Poynter, 1836-1919, is in the Walker Art Gallery, Liverpool.)*

The first poem I learnt was:

> "Wendy cracked a walnut,
> Threw the shell away.
> Crept a little pixie up to where it lay.
> 'Just the boat I wanted' Wendy heard him say,
> 'Thank you little Wendy' and he sailed away."

Another favourite rhyme was

> "Elsie Marley's grown so fine,
> She won't get up to feed the swine,
> But stays in bed till 8 or 9,
> D'ye ken Elsie Marley."

Miss Archer's was the next class. Each day she asked us if we had looked at the weather cock on the church steeple to check which way the wind was blowing. She was an attractive dark-haired lady who wore make-up and was very fashionable — when going shopping she often wore a hat, usually one with a veil and flowers, and seemed particularly fond of the colour pink. I believe that her fiancé had been killed in the first world war. We learnt to cut out material, to sew, and to embroider babies' bibs and aprons.

We progressed into Miss Gibson's class where she exercised strict discipline whilst skilfully teaching us history and English, firing my childhood imagination. She vividly described our Civil War and Cromwell. Regarding the colonisation of America we heard about the love story of John Smith and Princess Pocahontas. At another time we made an imitation of the Bayeux tapestry — on a long roll of strong white paper about 10" (approximately 25cm) wide we drew King Harold having his eye shot out with an arrow at the Battle of Hastings. Many story books were available, one being, the book "Waste Not, Want Not" — very apt for children during the spartan time of war. Miss Gibson did not hesitate to use the cane, a thin pliable stick about 2 foot (0.6096 metres) long, if one misbehaved. I had it once, for talking: it just caught the little finger of my left hand.

Quite unlike Miss Archer in attitude to dress, Miss Gibson, slim as a reed, never wore make-up, put her hair back in a bun, and usually wore a fawn-coloured blouse and cardigan with an ankle-length straight matching skirt and sensible, laced leather shoes which squeaked as she walked around the room. She rode a bicycle at least part of the way to school. Obviously a keen traveller, she once vividly described a holiday she had spent in Norway before the war sailing around the fjords.

The aforementioned 3 rooms had connecting doors. Access to Mr Irlam's classroom was from the outside. He was the headmaster and took the top class in which pupils were prepared for transfer to Rainford Secondary Modern School — where we already participated in Music Festivals singing songs such as, "Jerusalem" and "Nymphs and Shepherds" — or for scholarship entry to Upholland Grammar School. The previous scholarship transfer had been to Ormskirk Grammar School, prior to educational boundary changes.

The cane was used to punish anyone who misbehaved, for example, talking in class, fighting, or bullying other pupils. The nurse visited regularly to check on our physical health. Cheap milk was available and there were coal fires to heat the school. The curate, Mr Hodgson, who lived with his wife and baby in North Park Road, came to teach us religion, and thus we learnt the traditional form of the Creed. My mother taught us the Lord's Prayer and our nightly prayers as we knelt beside the bed — "This night as I lie down to sleep, I pray the Lord my soul to keep. If I should die before I wake, I pray the Lord my soul to take."

Within the school structure was School House occupied by Mrs Webster and her daughter, Miss Webster, who were the caretakers, and more. . . children who took eggs to school could have them boiled for lunch or dinners kept warm. My mother often walked down with chips in a bowl for my 2 brothers — Donald and Albert — and me. Next to the seniors playground on Old Rough Lane was the village policeman's house, and over another sandstone wall by Mr

Irlam's classroom was the Headmaster's House occupied by the McCoy family with its pretty garden. Mr McCoy had been headmaster from 1894 - 1929.

Across the road, opposite the seniors playground, was Mrs Atherton's cottage, set well back from the road — as were so many Kirkby dwellings — by a large garden. Here, with the help of her niece, Sarah, she sold sweets and lemonade. I particularly enjoyed dandelion and burdock which was a fizzy drink in a small dark-brown bottle. Bicycles could be left with them for safety, which is what most people did when going to dances at the Parish Hall, commonly referred to as the Village Hall, next door or to play football on the recreation ground behind the cottage.

There was a local dance band and the Village Hall dances were very popular with the adults, many people learning to dance by tuning in to the wireless (radio) to listen to Victor Silvester's instruction on ballroom dancing; waltzes, fox-trots, quick-steps, the Paul Jones, the rhumba and the tango. The villagers also enjoyed the old tyme dances; the lancers, St Bernard waltz, veleta, and the progressive barn dance. Refreshments prepared in a back room were served at the interval and included sandwiches, cakes — usually home-made — lemonade and tea. When my mother was a young woman, village dances were held in the school.

At village jumble sales, I particularly enjoyed spending my pennies on old-fashioned scrapbooks, because the cut-outs and postcards, Victorian/Edwardian in style, were so pretty. However, I did not regard as pretty at all the dress with a herring bone pattern which was bought for me at a sale for 2d when I was 4 years old, and I sulked whenever my mother made me wear it. 2d was the symbol for 2 old pennies, a penny being a large copper coin. 12 pennies made a shilling, which was a smaller silver coin, and 20 shillings made a pound, represented by a pound note, money commonly being referred to as "lsd". Local whist drives were popular with many villagers. For the children there were Christmas carol concerts and parties.

Wearing the 2d Jumble Sale Dress with cousin Roy Heaton

On the recreation ground there was a wooden pavilion, at the far end by the wood *(now the site of Ruffwood Comprehensive School)* and a huge roller stood at the side of it. This was used to keep the grass smooth for the cricket matches. It appeared to be quite a social asset to be a member of Kirkby Cricket Club and/or Tennis Club and/or Golf Club, this perhaps being a village reaction to the class structure so commonly identified with English society as a whole — upper, middle, and working class. The golf course was ploughed over during the war in order to provide more food for the community, (it has now been restored to its former use). In the winter time football was played on the rec', (and there was as much rivalry between our spectators and those from Rainford as there is now between the Everton and Liverpool fans!). My mother used to worry constantly about my brothers, especially Donald, who, when he had the opportunity, insisted on playing in goal.

Trespassers were warned to keep out of the wood at the behest of Lord Sefton's gamekeepers — Kirkby then still being an important part of his vast estate. His ancestral home was at Croxteth Hall, the family burial ground being in Kirkby churchyard. The Kirkby Tile Yard, where bricks were made, was situated off Ingoe Lane opposite the golf course (*a night club is now sited there*). Here a tenant could go to the office and request repairs. Twice a year farmers went to the Estate office at Croxteth to pay rent.

It was during the reign of Queen Elizabeth I, 1558-1603, that his ancestors, the Molyneux family, purchased Kirkby, and it was George III who bestowed the title Earl of Sefton in 1771. The land was valuable, being noted as some of the best farmland in south-west Lancashire. In 1811 out of the total population of 912 inhabitants, 130 families were employed in agriculture.

Apparently the last Earl of Sefton also had close connections with the British royal family for in the book entitled "The Windsor Story" there is a chapter on "The Cruise of the Nahlin" which includes a description of the uncrowned King Edward VIII's holiday in 1936 with his future wife — Mrs Wallis Simpson, an American divorcée, quote: "Several of

Church organists: Mr McCoy and Mr Bretherton

the King's old friends — Hugh Sefton and Foxy Gwynne (they met on the Nahlin and were married in 1941),. . . . ".
Also an American, this Lady Sefton, from all contemporary accounts, became very popular with Kirkby folk, and, with her mother-in-law — a lovely lady, who was not averse to giving schoolchildren a lift in her car if she passed them en route (as my brother Albert can vouch for) — often came on visits, perhaps to talk to the Mother's Union, recounting their visits to the poor in the back streets of Liverpool.

At the far end of the wood stood the house of the Church choirmaster, Mr Bretherton, Mrs Bretherton's father being Richard Hesketh (Richard Hesketh Drive was named after him). Their house was near to the site of Quarry Green, where American soldiers were stationed. It was later on, after the War with Germany had started, that the Japanese bombed the American fleet at Pearl Harbour on 7 December 1941 without any warning, and the following day Great Britain and the United States declared war on Japan.
At Bank Lane there was a battery of 6 anti-aircraft guns, which were manned by British soldiers who were accommodated in Nissen huts. The Airforce, R.A.F, was billeted at the Balloon Barrage in Field Lane, Moor End. A barrage balloon was a large balloon which was anchored to the ground with cables as a barrier against approaching aircraft.

Chapter II

Wartime innovations

The Forces

Double-decker buses started to run out to Quarry Green from the Fazakerley tram terminus. Girls from other villages and towns started to come to Kirkby in their hundreds hoping for a date with a *"GI"*, an American soldier — British soldiers were referred to as *"Tommies"*, Germans as *"Jerry"* or the *"Hun"*, Japanese as *"Japs"* and Italians as *"Ities"*. Anglo-American weddings flourished, courting couples being a common sight in the village. We schoolchildren were therefore exposed to 'the facts of life' but, apart from a girlish giggle and a boyish 'nudge, nudge', it seemed that that was all 'adult' stuff — our interests lay elsewhere, — in satisfying our wartime-starved 'sweet tooth'. *"Any gum, chum?"* and *"Babe Ruth"* candy bars became very much part of our childhood vocabulary. One day an American lorry went by and from the back of it a black soldier threw out oranges with a wonderful smile on his face, almost as big as ours as we ran forward to pick them up.

We had to carry gas masks to school and have training in how to put them on, and ear plugs were available to deafen the noise of the bombs and the anti-aircraft guns sited at Bank Lane. In the field across the road, opposite the infants playground, an air raid shelter was built and when we heard the sirens warning us of an air raid we were taken over there by our teachers. We would tell riddles — often carefully cut out from newspapers — and jokes and sing songs popular at the time like, "Run rabbit, run rabbit, run run run. . . " and "Roll out the barrel, we'll have a barrel of fun. . . " until the 'all clear' went again. That long, uninterrupted wail would rend the air and we would then come out again into the familiar Kirkby countryside. At home, in Glover's Brow, the original air raid shelter, which Dad had bought from the cement works at Netherton and sited under the ground at the side of the house, was replaced by an air raid shelter erected by the authorities outside our stable. Another was built over the road, a little further down towards Melling.

But air raid shelters; blackout curtains; no signposts; notices declaring "Careless talk costs lives"; — popular radio programmes like *"Worker's Playtime"*; *"ITMA"* — *It's That Man Again* — which starred the famous Liverpool comedian Tommy Handley; Vera Lynn, the Forces' Sweetheart, singing *"There'll be blue birds over the white cliffs of Dover"*; and Ann Shelton singing *"Lili Marlene"* — a German wartime love song — were all part of our daily lives. Other wartime innovations included petrol rationing, clothes coupons, sweet coupons, food rationing — people patiently queued for as little as one tomato — the black-market, ladies wearing turbans and snoods — a kind of thick, heavy hairnet which, although fashionable, also had a very practical safety purpose, to protect hair when working on factory machines — and painted their legs to look like they were wearing nylons which were highly prized black-market items.

Germany's main exponent of propaganda was the Nazi politician Joseph Goebbels, whilst "Lord Haw Haw," the traitor, William Joyce, an Anglo-American who was born in New York in 1906, broke into our radio wavelength to broadcast the Nazi propaganda from Germany with *"Germany calling, Germany calling"* to mock and try to demoralise. Instead of frightening us, we schoolchildren merely followed our parents' example and treated Joyce as a joke.

We always showed immense respect to both the King and

Grandmother Birch with my father

Queen by standing to attention even at home whenever the National Anthem was played on the wireless.

Familiar wartime jargon, (*word usage*), described the every-day experiences we children took for normal. It was no great surprise to us when relatives who were bombed out in Liverpool came to sleep on our kitchen floor or on chairs as make-shift beds. "Was Jesus bombed out?", was the question my little cousin asked his mother as they made their way from Aintree to the comparative safety of Kirkby. . . "because he had nowhere to sleep, did he, like us?" Their home at the Black Bull, Aintree, had been a direct hit, and auntie Sarah and uncle Billy Heaton arrived at our house covered in black soot, she carrying her baby daughter in her arms whilst her small son proclaimed to my mother, "Old Hitler's bombed us out!" Despite the dangers, my paternal grandmother, Granny, a widow — Grandad Leonard Birch,

Grandad Birch at home in Walton

a brass moulder at Fazakerley Signal Works, having died in 1932 — who lived in Lowell Street, Walton, declared "I won't move out of my home for old Hitler."

Another cousin, Harry, son of auntie Marion, Dad's sister, was evacuated for safety as were so many Liverpool children. He was sent to a school in North Wales. However, desperately homesick, he and another boy managed to find their way back to their homes in Liverpool, Harry to be greeted by his mother with the words: "And just when I'd sent you a food parcel!"

Of course we children thought it exciting to be called from our beds during the night and to go back downstairs when the sirens went, sometimes not to go out to the shelter, but to crouch under the kitchen table — my brothers almost driving my mother hysterical by playing dive bombers with their toy planes whilst she tried to steady her fraught nerves by eating an apple or knitting. My father would usually have been called out on Home Guard duty — meetings being held in the Village Hall. He had not been called up for the forces because his job as a supplier of milk was considered vital to the war effort. My mother tells the story that one night a white shape was seen in the field behind our house and, believing it to be a German parachutist, she called out the Home Guard — only to find that it was one of the local farmer's white cows! There was always this constant mixture of danger and humour in our lives.

And, of course, it **was** an exciting time and full of interest, especially because there were so many different people in transit. Any nationals of hostile countries, that is, aliens, were interned all over Britain. The Prime Minister, Winston Churchill, was particularly concerned about the possible existence of a 'Fifth Column' (an Organisation of European Nazi — German Socialist Party whose emblem was a swastika — sympathisers in Britain). There were several camps on the Isle of Man, including camps for women, Italians, Germans and Austrians.

In his book, "Beautiful Huyton with Roby' A Charming Residential Suburb", Andrew G. Colwell describes a Prisoner of War camp which was sited at Woolfall Heath, Huyton. It had a wire fence, eight feet (approximately 2½ metres) high, and was occupied by 2000 internees. Life inside the camp was said to be very difficult, 12 men sharing a house, each man being given a sack to stuff with straw and a 2 ounce (approximately 57 grammes) tablet of soap.

One night 2 French sailors, whose ship had been left stranded in Liverpool docks when France capitulated, and who were sleeping rough on Aintree racecourse, arrived at our door starving with cold and hunger. They quickly ate the bread my mother offered and gulped down pints of milk as we children watched, open-mouthed, and my Scottish grandmother repeated "Aye, aye" without understanding a word as they gabbled away to her in their native tongue.

German and Italian prisoners-of-war worked for local farmers.

One day, as I sat on the school wall, I saw a handsome blond man in a greenish-khaki uniform walking past, escorted by 2 British soldiers. Someone said that he was a German officer, probably in the SS.

From that same wall after the war with Japan ended in August 1945 we watched lorry loads of British soldiers, who had survived the atrocities of the Japanese prison camps, being returned from Japan, thin and yellowed, with quiet, seemingly slightly bewildered expressions on their faces as they looked at the children whose freedom, and democratic way of life, they had fought so bravely to protect. As we gazed back, equally quietly and questioningly, the one I noticed in particular was Raymond Watson, whose family lived at "Waverley" (now the local headquarters of Kirkby Conservative Club) in South Park Road. (A more recent hero, Simon Weston, writing about his experiences in the Falkland war in his book "Walking Tall", concedes that "The defence of freedom, I had discovered, is not cheap.")

Tragically my young cousin, Leonard Ford, a blue-eyed boy of 21, devoted to Granny Birch, and who had never been further than Liverpool and its suburbs, died in a Japanese prison camp from beri-beri. In his last letter home before capture he said the men were singing "Onward Christian Soldiers". One of his colleagues who survived said that Len remained defiant of his captors to the end, despite his suffering being made all the worse because it was believed that the Japs confiscated the Red Cross medical supplies. If this were true they contravened the Geneva Convention, an agreement made by the European powers at Geneva in 1864, which established the humane regulations regarding the treatment of the sick and wounded in war and the status of

Uncle Alex in Burma uniform

those who ministered to them. An indication of this special status was a flag or painted sign showing a Red Cross on a white ground which was prominently displayed on hospitals, hospital ships, ambulances and even on anyone attending the wounded.

My mother's 2 younger brothers served in the forces. Bill, joined the RAF and was posted to Canada, and Alex, a regular soldier, survived the war in Burma, but came home to suffer from malaria. He rarely talked about his time in the war, except perhaps to mention admiringly the leadership of Mountbatten, who had ordered: "Monsoon or no monsoon, we fight on." The Japanese did not, of course, expect the British army to fight on during those heavy daunting rains. (Churchill later wrote "The monsoon, now at its height, had in previous years brought active operations to a standstill, and the Japanese doubtless counted on a pause during which they could extricate and rebuild their shattered Fifteenth Army. They were given no such respite.") My uncle also spoke highly of General Slim. Occasionally he told my mother of the torment he and others had suffered — of watching a young comrade dying whilst calling out in anguish for his mother; about how, in the darkness, in the hot, steaming, jungle, they would hear a Japanese voice calling softly, tauntingly, in English, *"Tommy, Tommy. . . where are you Tommy? Come out Tommy"*, and of how a scout sent on ahead usually never returned.

A Kirkby son who did not return home was Bill Clarke, a family friend who had been a great help to my parents by occasionally helping to deliver the milk, and he had also installed the electricity in the air-raid shelter in our garden. He volunteered for the fighting services, and his willing spirit took him into the Royal Air Force, to become one of our heroic war pilots. His missions were over Germany: "If they ever tell me to bomb Berchtesgaten, Mrs Birch, I'll come over your garden!" he joked with my mother. Berchtesgaten was Hitler's mountain top retreat in Bavaria. Bill's 'plane, a Lancaster bomber, was shot down over Germany and he was killed. I remember his last visit to our house, with his girlfriend. He looked very handsome in his uniform. Bill, very solemn for once, remarked, prophetically, "You don't stand a chance in a Lancaster."

Chapter III

The Factory/Staff

Bombs were the instruments of death, just as were land mines, and Kirkby had a munitions factory. In August 1939, just before the war started, the Government, which had approved 4 new filling factories in the previous 4 years, decided to have 2 more, and sites were chosen at Risley and Kirkby. The villagers did not realise it then, but the "old" Kirkby, centuries old, was dying. The contractors moved into the area (now the site of Kirkby Industrial Estate) at the end of 1939, though the land was only formally purchased from Lord Sefton in 1943. The Government spent more than £8,500,000 on this Royal Ordnance factory. It filled 14 million shot for 6-pounder guns, and 20 million fuses for anti-tank mines, amongst several other orders. It employed more than 20,000 workers and, for them, Liverpool extended the old "19" tram route along the East Lancashire Road into the factory (now replaced by the "19" bus).

The administrative staff of the factory were housed close to it in Spinney Road (*these houses are still there*). To accommodate the workers — my mother's younger sister Henna worked there — who lived too far away to travel daily, a number of bungalow-type buildings were erected on 30 acres of land near the railway lines down South Park Road, commonly referred to as "the hostels". (After the war this property

Aunt Henna wearing typical hair-style and make-up of the 1940s

would, in turn, become an Emergency Teachers' Training College for recently demobbed servicemen; then, in later years, a Malayan Teachers' Training College — under the Federation of Malaya, its flag flying there — and, under the government of Liverpool Education Committee, Kirkby Fields Training College, which was opened in January 1963 for women student-teachers only.) (*The site is at present derelict land.*)

In the centre of the hostels was a cinema, which was a big thrill as the nearest other cinema, the Reo, was at Fazakerley. For 6d (2.5p), a child, accompanied by an adult — in my case, my long-suffering mother, as I loved going to the pictures at the slightest opportunity — could go to the hostel cinema and see a popular, up-to-date film starring, for example, Betty Grable, a glamorous Hollywood pin-up famed for her blonde hair and legs, her picture being on many of the 'planes leaving these shores on bombing or fighter missions abroad.

Another film favourite was Carmen Miranda, a South American lady who wore fantastic turban-like hats piled high with all kinds of fruit and flowers, and sang songs such as "I, I, I, I like you very much. . . " as she wiggled and danced on the stage, with a great smile on her face.

There were 2 houses on Thursdays and Sundays, one at 5 pm and one at 7 pm. The seating was provided by ordinary wooden folding chairs, all on the same level, so, if someone taller sat in front of me, which, not surprisingly, often happened, I immediately complained to my mother and we would then move to another seat. (I once heard films described as "the fairy stories of the 20th century" which I think is apt because of the enormous pleasure they have given to millions of people.)

Next to the hostels, 200 houses were built for the families of the key men brought from Woolwich Arsenal, and for those of the firemen employed at the factory. The doors of these flat-topped houses — roofing materials being then in short supply — were painted according to the vital war-effort job held by the occupier, in order that in emergencies the necessary type of worker could easily be identified and notified. (*These houses still remain, refurbished — no longer flat-roofed*).

These new families meant new friends and not only did they quickly and easily become part of the local community, they brought much pleasure, happiness and excitement with them, personifying the camaraderie spirit which was the ethos of the British nation during the war, that is, pulling together, especially through music and laughter. At the top of Mount Road a community building was set up which soon became known simply as '*The Hut*', and it was here that many socials, beetle drives — a dice and drawing game — and dances were held. There were also concerts, one being performed by the newly-formed youth club of which my brothers were members. One evening they performed a sketch on the German Chancellor/Fuhrer, Adolf Hitler, (Albert), and Benito Mussolini the Italian dictator, (Donald), which had the audience roaring with laughter.

At school, when it was suggested that hot dinners could be brought direct from the factory, our parents thought it a wonderful idea. However, the food was definitely not to our country taste and several children quickly abandoned the idea and, where it was possible, started to go home at lunchtime, I being one of them, there now being the aforementioned bus service between Quarry Green and the station en route to Fazakerley.

Chapter IV

Alick's House Farm

As previously mentioned, this bus service only started during the war. When I first started school I had to walk just over a mile, between school and home, our house, Alick's House Farm, being one half of a semi-detached property, Alick's House, in Glover's Brow, close to the Melling border. In those days mother could see the Liver Buildings from her bedroom window. The house is marked on 1845 and 1893 ordnance survey maps, and the name often arouses curiosity in people of my acquaintance but, to date, I have been unable to trace its origin; an archivist at Preston County Hall once suggested there might be a link with the meal trade.

Alicks House June 1963

Our House 1989

Small side garden at home

Mother and Father's Diamond Wedding

The original house had been a thatched dwelling which had burnt down at the end of the 19th century. A little of its sandstone remains at the base of one of our front garages. My parents, William and Bethia Birch, had been living in Netherton and moved in during January 1936, as did their neighbours, Mr and Mrs J R Bullen — he being an estate worker for Lord Sefton.

I was lucky as I had my brothers to take me to school. No doubt they were pleased when my confidence grew and I could go without them — they with their friends and me with mine — but in the beginning we went together.

When we left our mother on a Monday morning, usually after a breakfast of "*pobbies*" — boiled bread, sugar and milk, which also proved to be a soothing poultice after a tooth extraction — she would usually be preparing for washday. This involved lighting a copper boiler in the wash-house which was in the back yard. Initially the clothes were put into a galvanized washtub and my mother would then use a wooden *dolly-peg*[1] to make sure everything was thoroughly soaked. She then used a *rubbing board,*[2] followed by a good scrubbing to remove the stubborn stains. The clothes were then put into the boiler, before being rinsed — a *dolly-blue*[3] for the whites being popped into the water — in a tinbath, above which mother had a small Acme hand-wringer.

As she hung out the washing in the back garden a farm worker named Joe Morgan used to call out to her as he ploughed the back field with a horse and plough: "Spring-time, Mrs Birch", irrespective of the season! Household rubbish that could not be safely burned on the coal fire or on a garden fire was carried down the cartroad to the tip at the back of Mill Farm as no binmen called to collect. There were plenty of blackberries down the back fields, growing along the banks of the ditches — it gave one a sense of achievement to jump over a ditch and land safely on the other side. My mother and I used to enjoy taking the dog for a run down the back fields. We once found a wild duck's nest in the river bank. Further upstream, towards Bank Lane, beyond the small stone bridge, and standing on the slope of a field, was a straggly copse of tall trees (*still standing*) the one at the top of the slope always striking me as rather magical, as a small rivulet of water sprang from its strong roots and trickled down the slope into a small pool, on the side of which grew a marsh marigold.

Clothes were rarely, if ever, hung out to dry on a Sunday. Clothes pegs were often hawked round by local gipsies, who

1. **Dolly Peg:** A wooden pole with circular wooden base and 3 legs (*similar to a 3 legged stool with a pole protruding out of the centre*) used to pound the clothes.
2. **Rubbing Board:** Clothes were rubbed up and down its ribbed surface.
3. **Dolly Blue:** A muslin bag approx 1 inch cube containing a deep blue dye which was immersed into the water during the wash and had the effect of enhancing the whiteness in clothes.

often made a housewife nervous by warning her that unless she bought something from them, a curse would fall on her house.

As washing took so long to do, ironing was usually done on a separate day. The heavy metal flat-irons were heated at the coal fire — mother had 2 so that as one was being used, the other was getting hot. She held them with a padded cloth as the handles were very hot. The oilcloth-covered wooden kitchen table had a sheet spread over it and served as an ironing board. Shirt collars, then sold separately from shirts, were stiffened with starch, and this was mixed ready for use before ironing them.

When ironed the clothes were hung up to be aired on the rack — 2 wooden planks suspended from the kitchen ceiling in front of the fire. This was set in an iron and steel fireplace which had to be black-leaded with 'Zebo'' polish once a week to give it a shine, which was kept up with a daily dusting and polishing. It had an oven in which mother baked delicious scones. On the wooden ornamental mantelpiece, at either end, stood 2 bronze statuettes, each depicting a man holding a rearing horse by the reins. On the left-hand side of the fireplace was a big armchair known to the family as "Daddy's chair", and on the wall on the right-hand side was an 8-day Vienna wall strike clock, given to my parents by grandma and grandad Mattocks as a wedding present — these clocks were very popular after the first world war. In front of it was my father's rolled-top wooden desk, at which he often sat with his shirt sleeves rolled up, caught by arm bands, his black shiny waistcoat covering the upper part of his back as he worked on his round books and accounts. We often helped him to sort out and count the copper and silver change prior to his taking it to the National Provincial Bank Limited at the Black Bull, Aintree, (now National Westminster Bank plc).

Coconut matting covered the linoleum on the kitchen cement floor, the parlour having a wooden floor and being carpeted. When we had a party the mats were lifted so that the adults could dance better to the records played on our His Master's Voice radiogram. Sometimes my brothers and their friends had boxing matches in the kitchen or played darts, fastening the dartboard to the pantry door. Other games included tiddly-winks, snakes and ladders, draughts, and snap with playing cards. Wooden kitchen chairs with moulded seats, one tipped up against the other, became a make-believe horse and chariot. Pillow fights were great fun at bedtime.

My mother — whilst taking an active part in the running of the dairy business as a whole — particularly enjoyed helping out with the poultry. The hens were always ready to be let out early morning to scratch and clean themselves in the light soil. They wandered in and out of the henshed freely all day long to lay their eggs in nest boxes, which consisted of a row of sloping boxes attached higher up on the side of the shed, with wire bottoms on which straw was placed, and a narrow ledge ran along the front of them. At night they roosted on perches on a dropping board.

My father's favourite breed was the Rhode Island Red which laid a brown egg. We were always wary of a hen when broody as she would ruffle up her feathers and peck if one tried to feel under her to check the condition of the clutch of hatching eggs during the 21-day incubation period. We were also on our guard when walking near the cock as he was fiercely protective of his hens and would fly and fiercely peck any intruder. Rats were a problem, especially with the baby chickens — poison or the gun being used to kill them. Duck eggs were especially vulnerable when seagulls were overhead.

Of course some poultry would be killed at Christmas — my mother, Grandfather Mattocks, and Donald and Albert usually being the pluckers working in the wash-house where a fire was lit for warmth. Feathers would be floating everywhere. I usually watched my father cleaning and dressing the fowl in the pantry, ready for selling on the milk-round.

Albert at field gate with Bruce and Martha, our pet white duck

One Christmas Eve a pure white duck escaped her intended demise because a customer cancelled the order. After that no-one had the heart to have her killed and Donald named her "Martha" — perhaps in honour of Granny Birch? Martha lived on for another 13 years as a family pet and would greet us with a "Quack, quack" each morning as she made her way down to scrupulously wash herself at a dripping tap at the bottom of the garden near the midden. She survived a long, bitterly cold winter only to die on the first day of the following spring.

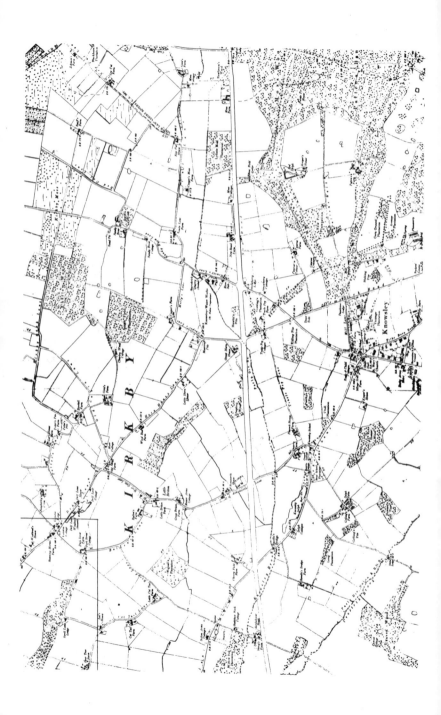

Chapter V

Local interests around home
The winter of 1940 — The death of Grandad Mattocks

As we came out of our big yard we sometimes saw a threshing machine on its way to a local farm. Crossing over to the footpath on the other side (*today there is a footpath on both sides of the road*), we walked alongside the high hedge which bordered Mr and Mrs Tuddenham's large garden (*approximately 12 houses now stand here*) — he was a gamekeeper for Lord Sefton. I once accompanied Mr Tuddenham to Kirkby Moss, off North Perimeter Road, to buy blocks of peat (*peat is still sold there*). Tuddenhams' dwelling and outbuildings included an outside ash toilet which was the householder's responsibility, a pig sty, and a coal place. There were 2 barns and storage buildings used by Mill Farm which was occupied by Mr Jim Rimmer in Mill Lane. (The opening of the property was approximately where North Mount Road opening is now). Prior to Tuddenham's occupation, Mr and Mrs Jim Roberts lived there at Glover's Brow Farm. Mrs Roberts kept a small sweet shop and often gave me the 'bottom' of the coconut candy jar.

Next to one of the barns was a black painted wooden caravan which was used as a holiday home by Nurse Lewis and

Grandma Mattocks

Nurse Perry, who both worked at Walton Hospital. At the bottom of the garden Tuddenhams kept poultry, hens being a common sight on most Kirkby homesteads, as were a couple of pigs.

Killing a pig was a common occurrence, the deed being carried out by Mr Harry Woods who lived in Hall Lane, Simonswood. Before his arrival my mother usually took me down to my Scottish grandmother's house in Melling. My maternal grandparents, Bethia and James Mattocks, had moved south from Glasgow, Scotland, to England as a young married couple where better employment was to be found. He was a skilled potter and the Midland Pottery was close to the Liverpool-Leeds canal in Melling. Here they raised 10 children, 5 boys and 5 girls — sadly, 2 other baby girls died.

Mother took me to grandma's house so that she and I may avoid the pig-killing event: we would walk down the pads, a footpath which cut through the fields between Glover's

Grandfather Mattocks

Brow and Waddicar Lane, Melling. There was a small swing-gate at the Kirkby end and a stile at Melling. Celendines and buttercups grew in the ditch which came after the border. It was tempting to pick a buttercup and hold it under a friend's chin to see if the latter liked butter, this being in the affirmative if a yellow glow reflected from the flower onto the skin. Dandelions were not picked when in full flower as it was feared that they made one wet the bed, but when in seed they were picked and children told the time by counting how many puffs it would take to blow away their white fluffy heads. Charles Hardwick, writing in 1872, in his book "Traditions, Superstitions and Folk-Lore" commented, "I know not whether the dandelion can be classed among the lightning plants, but I remember well the blowing away of its ripened winged seed with the view to ascertain the time of the day, as well as to solve much more profound mysteries." Daisy chains were a great favourite with the girls, as they had been during my mother's childhood.

Blackberries grew in profusion down the pads. In springtime there were catkins and pussy-willow on the trees by the large pit, on which green, slimy weeds were spread out — my mother would warn us that "Jenny Greenteeth" would get us if we went near the pit. Hardwick commented, "I remember well, when very young, being cautioned against approaching to the side of stagnant pools of water partially covered with vegetation. At the time, I firmly believed that, if I disobeyed this instruction, a certain water 'boggart' named 'Jenny Greenteeth' would drag me beneath her verdant screen and subject me to other tortures besides death by drowning. This superstition is still common in Lancashire." However, we would still attempt to collect frog spawn during the relevant season!

Springtime was especially welcome after the bad winter of 1940 when the milk had to be delivered on sledges over snow drifts 6 feet (1.8288 metres) high, and the menfolk dug their way out of Kirkby to Fazakerley to buy bread. Dad, always quick to take the chance to ride a horse — he once won an amateur horse race in Melling — rode to Fazakerley, choosing to travel over the fields where there was less snow.

Dad with Bruce 1940

Dad, Frank Owen, Donald and Alan Matthews 1940

During that bitterly cold winter when the milk had to be taken out by sledge — Donald and 2 friends from Melling, Alan Matthews,whose farmer father, Mr Thomas Matthews, produced milk at Wadacre Farm and was a supplier to my father, and Frank Owen, helping out — our grandfather Mattocks, who had been a great help with the pigs and poultry, and generally around the place — he painted the stones along the garden border from the front gate to the front door white to help us find our way during the blackout — took ill and died. Like grandmother, he had never lost his Scottish accent. He had been my best friend — making me 'rabbits' out of his red-spotted handkerchief, and letting me 'help' him to mix the meal for the pigs — it was a childish pleasure to put my hands in that sloppy mixture! Sometimes he would discipline me at the table for not eating my crusts. He would eye me affectionately with his large dark eyes above his droopy moustache, proclaiming: "You'll never

Grandfather Mattocks holding bucket used to make pig feed circa 1937/8

have curly hair if you don't eat your crusts!'' Sometimes he looked at me questioningly when a clean plate met his gaze, he being fully aware that the kitchen table had a wide shelf underneath, this proving a useful hiding place for the unwanted crusts!

Thus, as well as wartime dangers — and, although it seemed Britons did not believe it would happen, there was nevertheless a very real threat that Germany could win the war, that we would be conquered and put into concentration camps — the family at Alick's House Farm, like their fellow countrymen and women, experienced the private troubles that occur in the normal run of life and upset the routine of work, and the emotions.

Chapter VI

Start of walk to school
Dr Ainsworth — Women at war

Walking in the direction of the station, we passed on our left tall fir trees (*one still standing*) in front of our neighbours', Mr and Mrs Tinsley's, cottage. Mrs Holden lived with them in the part nearer our house. This was entered by a small white-painted wooden gate from the road which led to a front porch. A little further on was the plain wooden gate from which a large step descended into Tinsley's yard and outbuildings. They were surrounded by 2 large orchards in which grew, apples, pears, raspberries, blackcurrants, gooseberries, holly — its red berries making it a welcome Christmas decoration — and sweet-smelling yellow honeysuckle. There was a small greenhouse in which they grew grapes. Bantam hens and cocks strutted freely amongst the trees. One orchard was next to our big yard and the other bordered on Woods' orchard.

Occasionally, Mr Hesketh would be sweeping the road — he kept the local roads spick and span. He was a charming gentleman who sometimes gave me "birds' eggs" sweets to suck on the way to school.

At Woods' garage, nailed on a wall, was a green and black enamel "Raleigh" bike advertisement, depicting a man riding a bicycle. Out of school we had fun at the garage watching the big boys walking on stilts or riding a penny-farthing — an early type of bicycle with an overlarge wheel at

The Smithy, Glovers Brow 1989

the front and a very small one at the back, thus giving the cyclist a very high perch from which to look down on the rest of us. These activities, as well as roller skating and rolling wooden hoops, usually took place on the road as motor traffic was quite infrequent. We often felt safe enough to step into the road to press down bubbles left on newly laid tarmac.

At the end of the garage building was a smithy, (*still standing*) one of 2 in Kirkby I remember — the other being Mawdsleys' next to Running Horses Farm where Mr and Mrs Newsholme lived with their 2 children, Gert and Harold, and Mrs Newsholme senior (*near the junction of Simonswood Lane and Park Brow Drive*). I was lucky to be able to go sometimes with my father or Donald in the horse and float to Newsholmes' to collect milk. Besides enjoying the ride, especially enjoyable in late summer when we passed fields of waving golden corn and pretty gardens in which grew sunflowers and hollyhocks against cottage walls, it was also very pleasant to play in the barn whilst waiting for the milk tanks to be filled and loaded.

Mr Abraham, who lived in one of Kirkby Row cottages (*still standing*), worked in Woods' smithy. As we walked by on our way to school he, of a smallish but strong stature, would usually be busy heating up the coals, his face, like them, all red and glowing, preparing to shoe the horses and carry out other blacksmith's tasks: he always had a smile for us.

Opposite the garage was a large detached house divided into two (*now the site of Mill View flats*). The property was surrounded at the front by a sandstone wall about 6 feet (1.8288 metres) in height behind which were well-kept gardens. Just behind the wall was a big horse chestnut tree (*still standing*), which provided us with conkers in the autumn as well as an abundance of fallen leaves of red and gold through which we would scrunch our feet in happy childhood abandon, perhaps at another time having been 'flying' sycamore wings dropped by the tree nearer our home, enjoying that wonderful freedom of the country child.

Behind the wall nearer to North Park were pink-flowering hawthorn trees (*still standing*), unlike the then more common white-flowering hawthorn hedges around the Kirkby fields — the latter having significance in folklore. Hardwick commented: "The practice of gathering hawthorn blossoms, where practicable on the 1st of May, still continues, and in many localities superstition lingers respecting the supernatural properties of this tree." Other common Kirkby wild flowers included, the foxglove; red campion; marsh marigold; daisy; bluebell; coltsfoot; vetch; forget-me-not; and the beautiful, sweet-smelling white Dog rose (*we still have 2 bushes in our garden and no other rose smells as sweet to me*). Types of tree included, oak; elm; beech; lime; elderberry; box and yew. Bird life included the thrush; blackbird; robin; wren; sparrow; starling; swallow; blue-tit; crow; peewit; cuckoo; and, probably most folk's favourite, the skylark. Visiting seagulls always appeared like magic whenever there was ploughing.

The aforementioned property opposite Woods', on the Glover's Brow side, was called 'The Nook', this part of the

Dr Richard Ainsworth

house being occupied by Mr and Mrs Firth — he travelling by train via Wigan to work as a bank manager in Manchester. The other half of the house, on North Park Road, was called "Sunnyside" and was occupied by Mr and Mrs Stubbs and their daughter, Enid.

Glancing down North Park Road as we crossed over to the Carters Arms public house (*still standing*), in which lived Mr and Mrs Taylor and their family — mother sometimes sent us there for a tin of Smith's crisps, in each packet of which there was a tiny blue bag of salt — I would sometimes see Mr and Mrs Gregson, who lived in Chatham House halfway down North Park Road on the left-hand side (*now the Convent*). Mr Gregson later became Lord Mayor of Liverpool.

Lytham House (*still standing*), the home and surgery of Dr Richard Ainsworth, was down there on the right-hand side — he was the only doctor in the village. A brilliant man,

Lytham House, North Park Road

educated at Pembroke College Cambridge, and later The Middlesex, rumour had it that he could have had a Harley Street practice in London but felt that his calling was amongst the farm labourers, several of whom reported that he rarely asked for their bills. My mother says that he said the air of Kirkby was amongst the purest in the country. Whilst I was in awe, and slightly frightened, of him, nevertheless I greatly respected him. I always believed that he could cure any illness. (My mother recounts a relevant anecdote concerning Donald, when a small child. He came home one evening to report that, whilst playing, he had developed a headache and had just popped in to see Dr Ainsworth and when mother asked him what had happened, Donald simply replied that the doctor had given him a powder and it had gone better!)

Apparently acting as his own receptionist, Doctor usually went round the waiting room, which was in a wooden outbuilding at the bottom of the stone steps which led up into the surgery, quickly asking each patient's name. I remember one evening, after the War had finished, a 'displaced person' — in the early post-war years a camp was set up in Kirkby at Swell Lane for displaced persons, these being people from Eastern Europe mainly — gave a very long name and doctor said brusquely "Oh, I'll never remember that!" and moved on to the next patient, leaving the man looking after him with a mixture of bewilderment and fear on his face, but I knew well, suppressing a childish giggle, that he would probably receive the best treatment that he had ever had in his life.

To me, the displaced persons seemed a very serious, sad, people — such a contrast to the Americans — but now, on reflection, who wouldn't be? They had experienced the full horrors of World War II, having been subjugated both by the Germans and by the Russians, and were now uprooted from their native land, whilst we Kirkby folk still had our village, our county, our country, and were free to speak our native language. (My cousin, Monica Mattocks, who lived at Melling Mount, married a displaced person from Poland, later emigrating to Australia.)

At the Carters Arms we usually crossed back over the road to walk alongside Dearbolt delf, which we commonly referred to as "Woods' " delf, which was railed off. It was another place to play, and we would take risks by swinging from trees over an old quarry, the occasional victim immediately being rushed to Dr Ainsworth's for treatment.

Sometimes in the early days one would have to wait before crossing over the road whilst a herd of Rimmers' cows went past on their way from Mill Farm (*now the site of Mill Farm play school*), to graze alongside the railway lines, on the pasture down South Park Road, later the site of the hostels.

On the opposite side to the delf were 2 large semi-detached properties (*still standing*), these 4 houses being occupied respectively by Mr and Mrs Guest in "Inglehurst", Mr and

Mrs Smitton in "Stanley Villa", Mr and Mrs Roberts in "Pemberton Villa", and Mr and Mrs Manchester in "Homerlea" — their only child, Vera, was called up to the WAAFS — the Women's Auxiliary Air Force (*now Womens Royal Air Force, WRAF*).

WOMEN OF BRITAIN
COME INTO
THE FACTORIES
ASK AT ANY EMPLOYMENT EXCHANGE FOR ADVICE AND FULL DETAILS

Womanpower was vital for the war effort and on 17 March 1941 came the call for 10,000 women to do war work. The massive mobilisation plan was put into operation by Ernest Bevin, Minister of Labour, who declared the imminent registration of women, the aim being for them to fill vital jobs in industry and the auxiliary services. When it became necessary to enrol women aged between 16 and 49, who could then be compulsorily directed to other full time civilian employment, my auntie Phoebe went to make parts for planes at Napiers' factory, which was by the East Lancashire Road in Fazakerley (*now the site of the English Electric Co.*). My mother was exempt because she was helping my father in the supply of a food commodity.

By December women without children could be conscripted into the armed forces, for example, the WRNS — the Women's Royal Naval Service (*Wrens*), the ATS — Auxiliary Territorial Service (*now WRAC — Women's Royal Army Corps*), or the aforementioned WAAFS.

Women also played an active role in the ARP — Air-Raid Precautions.

Nursing, of course, was vital. Its inception in battle had been organized during the 19th century, on 5 November 1854, by Florence Nightingale. On 28 March 1854 Britain and France had declared war on Russia, known as the Crimean War, during which history records the Battle of Balaclava and the tragic Charge of the Light Brigade.

In his book "Conflict in the 20th Century" Charles Messenger states: "Thus the battle for women to establish equality with men took another stride forward during wartime, as the former demonstrated their capacity for hard work and bravery, for example, some of the greatest names in the resistance movements set up in enemy occupied countries during the Second World War were of women, who risked and faced the firing squad along with their male counterparts."

Chapter VII

Walk continued — Kirkby Railway Station
Wartime family treats

At the beginning of the war there was no roundabout (*as today*) between Manchester's house, "Homerlea", and the low-roofed building (*still standing*) used by the telephone exchange, next to which was the Railway Hotel (*still standing*). Hidden from our view was the hotel's excellent bowling green. The last house in Glover's Brow on that side was the home of the Powell family (*still standing*), Mr Walter Powell being a coal merchant. One of his sons, Noel, ran the local dance band.

At the end of Woods' delf we reached Roughley's sweet shop, at the back of which people, who had quite a way to travel to Kirkby railway station from Simonswood or Melling, often left their bikes. There was a red telephone box outside, where one learned to use the public telephone via the operator — to press Button A if your call came through or Button B to retrieve your money if there were no answer.

Then we passed the garden of the Station Master, Mr Hall. His house was the first in the row of Railway Cottages which were built on the slope leading down to the railway yard, these being occupied by Mrs Almond, who was the Station Master's mother-in-law, Mr and Mrs Pope and family, and Mr and Mrs Hill and family. The railway was privately

Kirkby Station circa 1910

owned, by the London Midland and Scottish Railway, the LMS — my brothers used to dare me to say a slight variance on the letters L-M-S, as the steam train 'panted' along so that it came out as "helluva mess, helluva mess", thus daringly swearing!

Over the railway bridge with its blackened sandstone wall we often glanced left in the direction of Wigan, towards the signal box, which was placed to give a good view of the line (with modern technology the boxes are no longer manually operated. One power box can cover an area formerly covered by 40 or more manual boxes).

There were 2 platforms, one on each side of the 2-track system. Passengers using the trains coming from Liverpool en route to Wigan and beyond would alight on the same side as the Railway Cottages, greet the ticket collector, and then climb up 2 flights of stone steps out onto Glover's Brow.

On the Liverpool side, a paved slope led up from the platform to the ticket office and the left-luggage room. In the waiting room on the platform there were seats, and on the walls there were pictures of far-away places, no doubt intended to inspire one to travel by train, as probably were the photographs posted in the fabric-seated single compartments of the steam trains in which was a mirror and netted luggage racks. Sometimes it was a corridor carriage. The Station Master and porter often opened the doors for passengers on arrival. In the Liverpool waiting room there was a coal fire: in the one on the Wigan side there was a stove. The platform gardens were always kept in good order.

I enjoyed going shopping to Liverpool, especially to the book shop called Philip Son & Nephew Ltd. in Whitechapel, or to Blackers store with its famous rocking horse or, nearer to home, to Irwins and the Creamery, both grocery shops by Fazakerley station. Bombed buildings in the centre of town did not deter our outings. Even if the sirens went en route, although there was the option to alight at the next railway station, we usually stayed on the train to its final destination, Exchange station in Tithebarn Street.

New Brighton in its heyday

Southport Outing: Cousin Monica, Albert, Donald, Dad, Irene

A rare treat was an outing to New Brighton. From Tithebarn Street we would almost run down to the Pier Head, and onto the Landing Stage — I can still feel the wooden planks moving beneath my feet and hear the thump, thump, of other people's feet as well as my own. At New Brighton there was the excitement of seeing the fairground, building sand castles on the beach, and paddling amongst the rock pools under the pier. All too soon it would be time to catch the boat and train for home, arriving back at Kirkby station very tired but very happy.

A rarer treat happened when our parents picked us up from school in Dad's small black Ford 8 de luxe car during the light nights to take us to Southport, mother bringing a flannel to wipe one's face and hands. Dad's car, which he had bought for £74 second hand, had a wireless, which was in those days a rarity. Dad usually stopped en route for us to eat the sandwiches mother would have prepared — gloriously happy outings. Once Donald spent all his allowance for the outing — 10s.0d. — on 10 consecutive rides on the big dipper!

Mother, Irene, Albert, Donald at Southport

An even rarer treat was an outing to Blackpool. The Chamber of Horrors in Madame Tussaud's Waxworks was a frightening experience, which we followed up by reading the tales of murder and horror from a souvenir booklet on the way home.

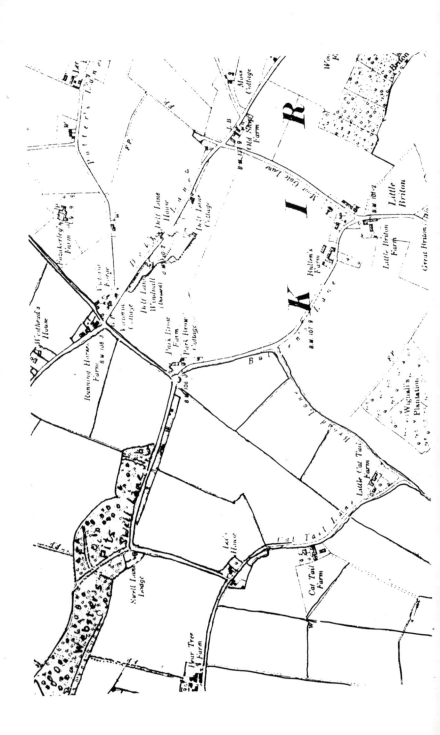

Chapter VIII

Walk continued
St. Chad's Church

Over the railway bridge we passed on our left The Cottage (*still standing*) the home of Mrs Spinks and her sister Mrs Ball. Turning left into Kirkby Row we crossed over to the footpath on the other side of the road, by Row Farm, the home of Mr Fred Mercer. His nearest neighbours towards Fazakerley — we used to recite the following in order to remember how to spell that name: "Mrs F, Mrs A, Mrs Z – A – K, Mrs E, Mrs R, Mrs L – E – Y" — along Shaw Lane, the road my mother used to refer to as "Kirkby Highway" (*now Whitefield Drive*), were at Pigeon House (*monument and "Whitefield House" still standing*). Ashcrofts farmed here — they too delivered milk. Their neighbours opposite were Popes who were farmers (*farmhouse still standing*) and, further along Ingoe Lane, on the right-hand side, was the cottage occupied by Miss Archer and her mother.

During the war people from Liverpool could be seen running along this road in the evening to seek shelter. Anywhere would do, — under hedges and in barns — in order to avoid the nightly bombing of the city, returning in the early morning to try and carry on their normal lives. At other times townspeople used it when coming out to find potato picking or pea-picking jobs on local farms.

Row Farm had an open barn (*approximately where there is now a bus stop, by Cotton Way*) opposite Kirkby Row cottages, in one of which lived Mrs Tyrer and her daughter, Elsie. They made black puddings which Elsie carried around in large baskets to sell.

A few yards after the cottages on the same side (*near the site of Poplar Drive*) was the village Post Office, the home of Mr and Mrs Allatt, their daughter Sarah becoming the village postmistress. There were stone steps leading up to the house.

Further along, on the opposite side (*close to where Holy Angels school is sited*), was a semi-detached property, set well back from the road by long paths. A school friend, Peter Hesketh, lived in the second of the 2 cottages with his parents and brother. The footpath was on that side of the road.

About 50 yards along, on the left-hand side was the home of the Rose family (*approximately just past Rowan Drive*) with its long garden along which extended a sandstone wall (*part still*

Kirkby Row, Sefton Cottage and Church

Kirkby Old Parsonage circa 1790 (later Beech Villa)

remains) — sandstone in any form is usually a 'clue' to old Kirkby sites. On the same side was Sefton Cottage (*still standing*) with its spacious lawns.

Opposite Sefton Cottage, was Beech Villa (a postcard depicting it in earlier times states that it was originally the parsonage), which probably took its name from the beautiful, gigantic copper beech tree (*now chopped down*) which stood majestically on the lawn at the corner of the road.

As we crossed over, we usually glanced down the road to the right, (*now James Holt Avenue*) to the area known as The Shroggs. Here was the tennis club (*now the site of Kirkby Home*), and, set among trees, were a few houses, in one of which lived Mr and Mrs Heyes.

Across the road from Beech Villa, on our left, was the property called The Cocoa Rooms, occupied by Mr and Mrs Brown and family. Mrs Walker, also lived there with her husband and baby daughter. She ran the local Brownie pack,

King George VI and Queen Elizabeth

being our Brown Owl. Meetings were held in a top floor room or, weather permitting, on the lawn outside. When King George VI and Queen Elizabeth visited Kirkby, another Brownie and I were instructed to stand at the side of the road by the recreation ground. As they passed by, the Queen glanced over with a smile and touched the King's arm. He, dressed in uniform, immediately looked in our direction, with a rather tense, serious, but, at the same time, gentle expression on his fair-skinned face.

Crossing the small sandstone bridge over Mill Brook (*both still remain*) we usually glanced down into the sparkling clear water in which we often paddled further upstream, towards Mill Farm.

On our right, built at the end of a long drive which stretched back through a wood towards the Lodge at Swell Lane, was the home of another Mr and Mrs Brown and family. They lived in the Lodge (*still standing*) opposite the lychgate of the church. His brother, Bob, was a particularly popular figure in

Bob Brown standing extreme left: Albert seated second from left

the village, especially because of his support for the local footballers.

Rhododendrons flourished in this wood. Although I rarely visited the Swell Lane area near Park Brow, where Mr and Mrs Rimmer occupied Park Brow Farm, nor Cat Tail Lane, Ribblers Lane where a schoolfriend, Beryl Rimmer lived with her two older sisters, Ethel and Lilian and their parents, Little Brook, nor Little Briton, I always enjoyed it when I did, especially because of the prettiness of those parts of the village and because of the famous Kirkby hospitality (which apparently still flourishes today — I recall a local newspaper reporter stating only a couple of years ago that one could always be sure of a cup of tea in Kirkby). I remember particularly the birthday parties held at Park Brow Farm to which my friend, Eileen Heyes, invited me, Mr Rimmer being her grandfather.

Miss Bessie Heyes at pump which served 6 cottages at Little Briton

St Chad's church was built in 1869-71 at the cost of the 4th Earl of Sefton with the free labour of his tenants in Kirkby and the nearby village of Simonswood, local sandstone being carried from quarries in Kirkby and Melling. The nave shows octagonal pillars on the left-hand side and round pillars on the right as it is said there was a dispute between the Simonswood and Kirkby farmers which is why in the years that followed the Simonswood farmers sat on the north side and the Kirkby farmers on the south side of the church. People called it *"Sefton's Folly"* because it seemed so unwise to have such a large church — it is sometimes referred to as *"The Country Cathedral"* — for a small community. In reply, it is said that this Lord Sefton prophesised that one day Kirkby would become a large town.

The prized Saxon font is described by Charles F Larkin in his Paper entitled *"The Kirkby Font"* in which he reminds us on p99: "When our font was in the making the great struggle between Henry II and Beckett had not long resulted in the archbishop's murder." An example of its figures is the *"Temptation of Adam and Eve"* showing Eve giving Adam an apple which he is receiving. The font thus dates Kirkby, as does the tradition that St Chad, Bishop of Mercia 669, visited the village.

When attending church, one of our Sunday School teachers, perhaps Miss Strong or Mrs Tinsley, drew our attention to the font and also to the beautiful stained glass window depicting Jacob's dream, and to the jewel-like mosaic reredos of the Last Supper.

In his book *"The King's England LANCASHIRE"*, Arthur Mee noted that "In the vestry stands a little model of the simple church before this one, carved by the village schoolmaster from a piece of alabaster left over from the pulpit; and outside in a graveyard trim as a garden is a modern cross to remind us that the Danes found a church here 1000 years and more ago." The stone from the old chapel, taken down in 1872, was used to build a wall around the new church.

Service on a Sunday evening was usually well attended. Women and girls were expected to wear a hat. A kind of social outing, it afforded the opportunity for villagers to meet together, and to stay behind for a talk, farmers would be discussing their crops, whilst their wives talked about the latest Mothers' Union outing, and many a romance started this way as young men and girls would stand chatting by the lychgate before setting off in a group to walk, often along the Church Fields in the direction of Mill Farm.

Walking alongside the graveyard wall we saw, on the opposite side of the road, the 3 searchlights used for spotting enemy aircraft. In the Vicarage (*still standing*) on our left, lived the Rev. and Mrs Griffiths and family of young men and women. Its wide lawn was often the setting for village Garden Fêtes — my brother, Albert, once winning a pig in a skittle competition!

Rev Griffiths with Kirkby Team 1951

On our way home from school we would sometimes run into the drive to pick up fallen crab apples from the tree by the Vicarage gates. As described in the 'Good Housekeeping' magazine for October 1989: "It has small pinky-white blossoms which open in May, followed by tiny 2.5cm (1 inch) fruit in the autumn. These are round and yellow, sometimes tinged with pink and always sour. . . . Remains of crab apples have been found in excavations of Neolithic lake villages in the west of England, and throughout the centuries they have been associated with magical powers. If you sleep under a crab apple tree, you might be carried off by the fairies, or more ominously, if you find a spray of blossoms among the fruit there might be a death in the family. In the West Country, girls would collect crab apples and arrange them in the shape of their sweethearts' initials."

Opposite the drive was a small road leading up to Kirkby

Hall farm (*now the site of Kirkby Council offices, the Kirkby Suite, and the Swimming Baths*) which was surrounded by large fields. It was the home of Mr and Mrs George Rimmer and their son and daughter. Their domestic help, Mary Tyrer, was a local girl — "going into service" being one of the few 'careers' available to the village girls in pre-war days.

We continued to walk on the only footpath, still on the vicarage side of Old Hall Lane, alongside a hedge, glancing over to open fields and 2 wooded copses on our left (approximately behind the site of the present Kirkby C of E Primary School and Old Hall Estate).

Finally we reached a well-built semi-detached property on our left at the cross-roads, set well-back from the road, with well-tended gardens at the front. In one house lived Mr and Mrs William Owen.

Opposite on our right-hand side, was a tall tree — I remember it well because the first few steps I took home alone without Donald, were as far as that tree! When he caught up with me, he gave me a 'big brother' rollicking for not having waited for him as told! It couldn't have been easy for him having a small sister to look after. On the Tuesday of my first week at school I burst into tears on seeing our greengrocer, Cyril Baker, who lived in Melling, passing by up School Lane (*now County Road*) without stopping — my mother always bought me a penny (1d) apple when he called at our house. Donald was brought from the senior play-ground to the infants to find out why I was crying. On hearing the reason, he, very maturely, explained that you didn't buy apples when you were attending school!

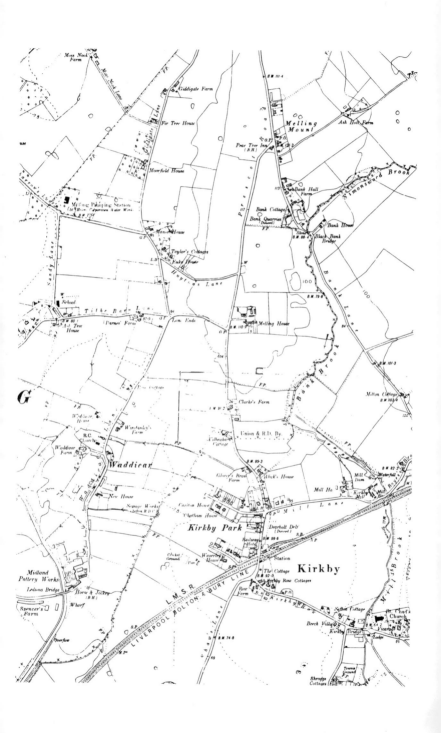

Moss Nook Farm

Moss Nook Lane

Fiddisgate Farm

Fir Tree House

Chapels Lane

Moorfield House

Melling Pumping Station
(St House Liverpool Water Works)

Manor House

Taylor's Cottages

Fold House

School

Tithe Barn Farm

Ash Tree House

Parnes' Farm

Lane Ends

B M 80·1

B M 37·9·3

B M 110

Melling House

G

Waddicar House

Winstanley's Farm

R.C. Church

Waddicar Farm

Waddicar

Waddicar Lane

New House

Sewage Works
Sefton R.D.C.

Midland Pottery Works

Leitons Bridge

Spencer's Farm

Horse & Jockey
(P.H.)

Wharf

Overflow

B M 111·4

Melling Mount

Ash Holt Farm

Pear Tree Inn
(P.H.)

Prescot

Simonswood Brook

Bank Hall Farm

Bank Cottage

Bank Quarries
(Disused)

Bank House

Stone
B M 88·

Black Bank Bridge

Haytons Lane

Bank Lane

B M 79·6

100

84

100

Bank Brook

B M 101·3

Milton Cottage
B M 103·4

Clarke's Farm

B M 91·2

Union & R.D. By.

Ashenham Cottage

B M 95·3

Glover's Brow Farm

Alleck's House

Mill Ho

Mill Dam

Waterfall

B M 82·2

Kirkby Mill

Mill

Carlton House

Chatham House

Kirkby Park

Dearholt Dely
(Disused)

S.B.

Railway Hotel

B M 99·6

Church Ground

Waverley House

Pav.

Station

The Cottage

Kirkby

B M 92·0

Kirkby Row Cottages

P.O.

Rose Farm

Kirkby Brook

Sefton Cottage

St Chad's Church

Brick Village

Kirkby Bridge

Lodge

65

LMSR LIVERPOOL BOLTON & BURY LINE

Causeway Lane

B M 74·8

49

Tennis Ground

Shrodgs Cottages (Fall Mill Ho)

Chapter IX

Walking home via Red Brow
Horse transport — Donald's accident

When I grew a little older, my mother arranged piano lessons for me with Miss Clegg, an elderly lady, who lived at the start of Bank Lane on the left hand side, next to the cross-roads (*where there are now traffic lights on Boyes Brow and County Road junction*), and so, on a Wednesday afternoon, I would take a different route home, in order to call at Miss Clegg's. I walked via School Lane with school friends who lived on the way, to the area known as Red Brow.

After the recreation ground we passed Heskeths' small-holding on our left, and Ruddins' Piggery on our right — this being managed by Mr Mellor who lived there with his family, the son, David, being a particular friend of Donald. Then we passed Mr and Mrs King's cottage and garden on our right, just at the top of the decline in the brow. On the same side, but lower down the dip, was the home of the Pickup family, a daughter, Olga, being especially known to my family as she later came to work — and to work very well — on the milk-round, helping Donald to deliver the milk with a horse and float.

In pre-war days, when competition between milkmen was extremely keen, my father had gone out twice a day because pasteurisation was not then in operation all over the country and milk went sour quicker. This method of distribution continued up till the outbreak of the war, when shortage of manpower and petrol rationing reduced the service to one delivery only, and the Ministry of Food decided to rationalise milk distribution at that time and thereby reduce competition between the distributors to the extent that only 2 milkmen were permitted to operate in any single area — this would probably have pleased the Irish writer, Bernard Shaw, who many years ago quoted the distribution of milk as being wasteful. Wartime savings in milk distribution were estimated at £2.25m per annum.

The present generation is essentially technology-minded and young people might find it difficult to imagine the horse as being considered as a rival to motor transport. However, its importance was very real years ago as the following extract from the July 1930 issue of "The Milk Industry" magazine helps to prove:-

"WHEN HORSE TRANSPORT IS ECONOMICAL"

"For several years there has been a marked increase in certain items connected with road transport, in particular the road tax and the petrol duty. This has proved a specially heavy burden on short distance deliveries such as milk rounds, owing to the high fuel consumption in terms of miles per gallon. The constant starting and stopping necessitated by calls at frequent intervals forces up the consumption to the highest point, the result being that a machine which gives 18 miles per gallon according to the maker's specification, works out in the actual practice in the neighbourhood of 7.

Where the weekly mileage covered does not exceed 100, it is very doubtful whether a motor vehicle is in all cases a paying proposition. During the last decade, the horse has regained much of the ground it had previously lost to mechanical transport, evidence on this point being recently tendered before the Royal Commission on Transport, when it was pointed out that whereas ten years ago the economic radius of the horse was only a mile and a half, today it has risen to something like five miles. Nor is the reason for this either obscure or difficult to find, being very largely due to the freedom from taxation enjoyed by the horse. It is, in fact, almost the only means of inland carriage to continue to have such an exemption. Moreover, the capital cost of even the most elaborate turnout is modest compared with any mechanical vehicle, with its expensive road licence duty and 4d./gallon fuel tax. In town and city work, there is not a great deal to choose between them, on account of the paralysing effect of traffic congestion which brings down the rate of travel of the fastest machine to that of the slowest. The question, therefore, arises whether it is really worthwhile to employ an expensive vehicle and pay the consequent government impositions, when there is such a small difference in the amount of work done. Little wonder is it that an increasingly large number of users of low mileage vehicles are turning again to the horse. It is purely a matter of value for money."

Another point in the horse's favour was that the animal knew the round as well as his master, and this knowledge proved useful, especially at Christmas when the driver had been celebrating at several of his customers' houses! Also, having myself had the difficulty of finding my way on a strange round, the fact that the horse knew the round must have been a great help to a new roundsman.

However, this ability once proved disastrous for Donald.

Although Donald was academically proficient at school, and at the same time had a talent for art — a manager from the Soap Works at Aintree once recommended that my parents send him to art school — he never wished to take advantage of a scholarship and attend a grammar school. Instead he thoroughly enjoyed his time at Rainford Secondary Modern School. All that he ever wanted to do was to help his Dad on the milk round, even pleading to be allowed to do so.

One morning in 1942 he was helping out on the Melling round. Suddenly the horse shied at a loud noise from a farm machine and bolted. Donald, noticing 2 little girls in the road, responded in his usual altruistic, responsible manner, showing a maturity beyond his years. Realising that they would be afraid, and perhaps in some danger, he hung onto the reins trying to control the frightened animal as it turned sharply into Woodland Road — its normal route. This action trapped Donald's left leg below the knee between the iron foot pedal on the milk wagon and a low brick wall. Although he had stopped the horse, he was badly injured, lying helpless in the road.

Dr Ainsworth was quickly called to the scene as was auntie Sarah who was then living with her husband and children with grandma Mattocks in Melling following the aforementioned bombing of their home. She accompanied Donald to Ormskirk hospital where it was decided to amputate the leg. Incredibly, the theatre sister noticed that, although the leg was only hanging on by ½″(approximately 12mm), the main artery was still warm, and thus there was a possiblity that the leg could be saved if Donald could be taken immediately to Fazakerley hospital.

The ambulance stopped briefly outside our house whilst Mum and Dad rushed out to comfort him, Donald, in return smilingly reassuring them. On arrival at Fazakerley, it was found that the main surgeon was not available. Instead, my parents received a telephone call from Dr Shackwell, a young, inexperienced surgeon who was blind in one eye. He promised them that he would do his best, that it was like an architect setting out to plan a building — the outcome was unknown. He described Donald's reaction to this news: "Don't worry, Doc, I can take it." Those brave words from a 13-year old boy inspired the young doctor and the leg was miraculously saved, although months of treatment were to follow. A couple of years later Donald received a letter from Dr Shackwell, who was then a soldier serving in Burma. He wrote that he had saved a lot of arms and legs since Donald's but he still regarded him as his prize case. (Many years later

N.B. for Dr Shackwell read Mr Shatwell

surgeon and patient were to meet again in peacetime when Donald went into Ormskirk hospital to have his appendix removed.)

Our milk customers on all rounds were very concerned about Donald, constantly enquiring about his welfare and bringing him gifts, for example, the Dutch de van der Shueren family who lived on Aintree Lane, Aintree, the father holding a high managerial position at the silkworks, the British Enka, on Ormskirk Road. After the war he and his family returned to Holland. (In the 1960s, prior to a visit to Amsterdam with my young sister, Ann, I attempted to contact our former customer. In reply I was informed that he had retired, and that my letter would be forwarded to his new address. One evening in Holland a messenger delivered a parcel to our hotel room: it contained a beautifully packaged box of delicious chocolates sent with Mr de van der Shueren's compliments, and a letter expressing fond memories of his association with our family.)

When his leg was sufficiently strong for him to walk again without the aid of his crutches, Donald declared that he was going to return to taking out the milk with the horse and float, much to his parents', especially his mother's, apprehension and fear. He won them over by saying that he had to get his nerve back, which he did, not only by returning to the job he loved but also by playing in goal for Kirkby football team. After a Saturday match he and his pals would cycle to the dance held at Rainford village hall.

I was 7 years' old at the time of Don's accident. It was a terrible shock to hear the news when I came home from school that night, to see my mother in tears, and my father almost the same but trying to hide his own grief in his attempt to comfort her. It seemed unbelievable that Donald could be in hospital, the victim of a tragic accident. Our family security, the 'safeness' of home, had been shattered, and I felt frightened, bewildered, and angry that life could deal such an unfair blow. (It is almost the same experience now that Donald has died, one of utter desolation, disbelief, and sadness, an awful shock to us all).

Dad on 'Lady' with 'Beauty' in pasture

When petrol was put on the ration during the war, milkmen had to look for suitable horses to pull their floats. My father went to various horse sales in North Wales. It was rather surprising that Dad found his way around so well as there were no signposts in wartime and at night there were no lights in the lanes of Kirkby. However, the sky over Liverpool was often red with the glows from fires caused by the bombing (one still reads about unexploded bombs being discovered in Liverpool. An article in the "Liverpool Echo", dated 12 February 1990, which is more than 40 years after the end of the war, reported one being found in Walton: and, nearer home, in the 1960s an unexploded hand grenade was found on our cartroad).

Dad was lucky in buying *"Beauty"* and *"Lady"*, both very popular horses with the customers and proving to be reliable and hard-working — unlike *"Bobby"*, a beautiful chestnut, but very temperamental. He hated work, ie, being put between the shafts, but he loved jumping! We enjoyed looking after the horses, treating them more like pets, feeding and grooming them in the stable when we used a curry-comb — a metal brush. We especially enjoyed riding them, for instance, at Ashtons' farm at Melling Rocks where Dad sometimes put them out to pasture. Beauty once threw me but I was soon up again and carried on riding. Dad complimented me on that and I felt very proud. It was probably female pride that made me do it, in competition with my brothers!

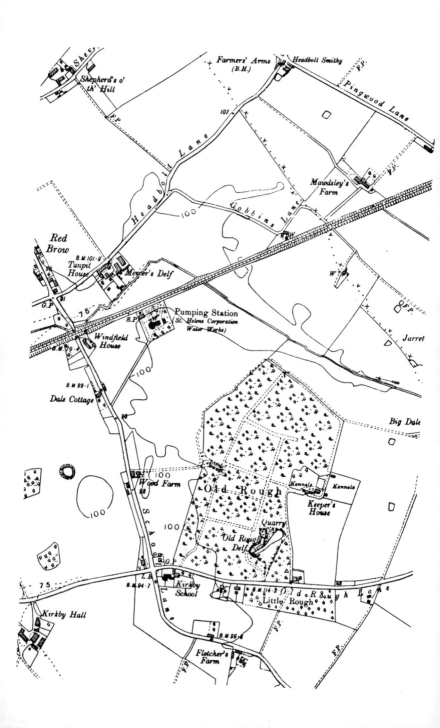

Chapter X

Walk continued
The Waterworks – Mill Dam – Accents –
Almost home

At Red Brow, across the fields behind Kings' and Pickups', one could see the then famous Kirkby "landmark", Kirkby waterworks, (now demolished, only a circle of trees surrounds its "grave"). This much-admired, and much-loved building — it was very exciting for a school-child to be taken to the top of it — had been modelled, it is said, at the wish of the Seftons, on beautiful Warwick Castle. One used to advise friends from the Wigan area travelling by train to Kirkby for the first time to look out for the waterworks on their left and then they would know they were arriving at their destination.

On our left were houses in which lived some of the most well-known Kirkby families, with the familiar names of Tyrer, Wilson, Woods, Davies, Rawlinson, Green — Mrs Green being my mother's sister Chrissie — Warburton, Fogg, Fyles, Molyneux, Morgan, Rimmer, Parkinson, Aspinall and Mather. Most of my companions on the walk to my music lesson lived here so, by the time I walked under the railway bridge (*still standing*), I was on my own for the last few yards to Miss Clegg's house.

Ann on wall by Red Brow pasture 1957

On the right was a pasture which belonged to Red Brow Farm, tenanted by Mr James Mercer. In winter time we used to make sledges out of wooden boxes and take a sleigh ride down that pasture slope, sometimes one of us losing control and landing up soaking wet in the brook at the bottom. There was a small sandstone wall alongside the pasture as it was higher than the road. The farmhouse and buildings were a little along Headbolt Lane on the right, (approximately sited opposite to, and between the present Heathfield and Fallowfield roads).

Crossing over to Miss Clegg's house, which she shared with Mr and Mrs Appleton and their 2 small children, the wife having formerly been Enid Diggles, whose family occupied Fletcher's Farm, just past the school, towards Running Horses and Delf Lane — Mr & Mrs Tyrer living in the cottage on the left nearer the school — I noticed the big house opposite, on the corner of Bank Lane and Headbolt Lane. Further along Bank Lane, on the right, was a row of 4 houses, in one of which lived Mr and Mrs Alan Quarry and family. Further along, on that side was a house occupied by

Mill Dam

Mr and Mrs Wilcox and family, and outbuildings used by Red Brow Farm. Next to them was the gun-site, and next to that, just before Shevington Lane, were 3 houses, in one of which lived Mr and Mrs Cheetham and family, their neighbours being Dorothy Giles and her family. She took milk out in a horse and float for Rimmers, Mill Farm. Everything else around was open fields.

After my music lesson — examinations were taken at Crane's theatre in Liverpool — I turned right into Boyes Brow, and passed 3 cottages on my right. There was another cottage on its own — a tithe cottage belonging to Mill Farm — in which lived another classmate, Brian Hull, with his family. By the time I reached the bridge by the mill, my mother had usually come to meet me. Glancing to the right we would see the waterfall cascading from Mill Dam, which often froze over during wintertime. We would skate and slide on it, never quite certain whether or not it would give way, sometimes even venturing up the frozen brook further upstream. But there were always the 'big' boys to look after us, like Donald and Ken Woods of the building family from Melling.

In the summer we would paddle in the brook by the waterfall and catch jacksharps. Mother would make us a fishing-net out of the foot of one her old stockings, which she would fasten onto a beanstick with a piece of wire. There were hundreds of jacksharps and when I went to bed at night and closed my eyes I could still see them! Once I caught a cat-fish in the water running from the mill — I was so frightened of its 'ugly' face I could hardly put it into my jam jar!

As we were walking home one afternoon, accompanied by our black and white sheepdog, Bruce, mother told me of the unnerving experience she had had that morning when walking home along Boyes Brow. A large German plane had swooped low, casting a huge dark shadow. A boy was passing by with a horse and cart and she and he had just looked at each other without saying a word. The plane had risen again and flown away. Shortly afterwards the sirens went. Mother heard later that it had been spotted over Birkenhead. Probably the pilot was looking for the docks there on the River Mersey.

Kirkby, having a factory and railway, was itself sometimes a target. One night the Germans dropped flares all around the factory. Fortunately, the bomber planes were spotted in the searchlights and the anti-aircraft guns opened fire. If the bombs had found their target that night, it is very doubtful that there would be any Kirkby left today on which to comment! Another time a bomb which fell in Kirkby Row near the Post Office leaving a deep hole, failed to explode and it was some days before the bomb disposal squad found time to defuse it. House windows were protected from the blast of the guns and bombs by brown paper strips pasted diagonally across the panes. We often saw strips of silver foil covering the roads and fields and were told this was dropped by the Germans in an effort to block out radar signals.

After we passed Mill Farm we passed 3 private houses on our right (*still standing*), in one of which, "Katanga". lived Miss Timms, the Girl Guide mistress, with her parents. Another "Beverley," was occupied by Mr and Mrs Jones and Mr Whitehead — he was particularly popular with local children because he gave us his old tennis balls. A family called Ross lived next door in "Clarehaven". Next came a Sefton semi-detached property. In the first house No3 lived Mr and Mrs James Holt, (James Holt Avenue was named after him) and their daughter, Lucy. Next door, in No1 with their family of boys and girls, lived Mr and Mrs Robert Woods, who ran the garage.

There were other houses in Kirkby which were privately owned, for example, by men employed by the famous Cunard shipping company, self-employed businessmen, or retired folk. Interestingly, some land in Glover's Brow had once been 'glebe' land, that is, parish land which belonged to the church.

It was not surprising therefore that the accents in Kirkby varied '— some local people spoke with a quite strong Lancashire accent/dialect, others less so, and then there were the clear, bell-like tones, spoken by Miss Sarah Atherton and Mrs Alice Wharton (*both still living in Kirkby*), all these contrasting with the accents of the outsiders who had come to live in the village, —the British soldiers, the factory workers, the Americans, and the aforementioned businessmen.

The following recitation, which I believe to be in the Northern dialect, was taught to me as a child by a school friend Evelyn Travis of Hall Lane, Simonswood. I have tried to reproduce it as it sounds as I cannot find a copy of the original.

A NICE CUP O' TAY (TEA)
Tha maunt cum on a Mundée
It's me washin day
I'll be washin an washin me cluess away
But if tha cums on reet day
I'll give thee a nice cup o' tay

Tha maunt cum on a Tuesdée
It's me ironin day
I'll be ironin and ironin me sheets away
But if tha cums on reet day
I'll give thee a nice cup o' tay

Tha maunt cum on a Wednesdée
It's me cleanin day
I'll be cleanin and cleanin me windows away
But if tha cums on reet day
I'll give thee a nice cup o' tay

Tha maunt cum on a Thursdée
It's me shoppin day
I'll be shoppin and shoppin me baskets away
But if tha cums on reet day
I'll give thee a nice cup o' tay

Tha maunt cum on a Fridée
It's me brushin day
I'll be brushin and brushin me brushes away
But if tha cums on reet day
I'll give thee a nice cup o' tay

Tha maunt cum on a Saturdée
It's me bakin day
I'll be bakin and bakin me pies away
But if tha cums on reet day
I'll give thee a nice cup o' tay

Tha maunt cum on a Sundée
It's me prayin day
I'll be prayin and prayin me sins away
But if tha cums on reet day
I'll give thee a nice cup o' tay

Just before reaching the delph at the top of Mill Lane we passed the large house "Hillside" (*still standing*) on our left. It was occupied by Mr Harry Ledson.

Laburnum Arch, Uncle Billy Heaton and me circa 1939

Then we turned right into Glover's Brow, almost home. In summer we could immediately identify our house by the yellow-flowering laburnum arch over our front gate, which, made of wood, was painted black and white and had pointed tips. Sometimes we went in through the big yard gate which was of a typical wooden field-gate design: there was a small stile between it and the stable.

Our house, also painted black and white, was surrounded by a privet hedge at the front and a thick hawthorn hedge at the sides and back. Behind lay open fields right across to Bank Lane. As aforementioned, a favourite walk led along the cart-road which stretched between the back fields from our big yard as far as the top of the field which bordered onto the brook at the bottom.

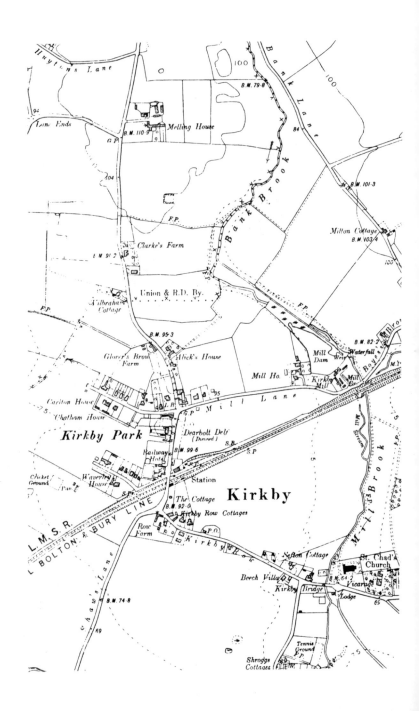

Chapter XI

Immediate Melling neighbours
Wilbraham Cottage—Clarke's Farm

Before crossing over I usually glanced left, down towards Melling, and saw Wilbraham Cottage which was on the left and was the first house in Melling, at the start of Prescot Road, just the other side of the ditch which formed the Kirkby/Melling border. It was a lovely, large red-bricked house, with a sweeping lawn on a semi-circular drive with well-established trees at the front. Between the ditch and the side of the house was a conservatory, and at the back was an orchard. Inside the house, a magnificent staircase descended into a large hallway, off which led various rooms.

The name "Wilbraham" is part of Melling history through Thomas Bootle of Melling. He represented Liverpool as a Tory in 1724 and 1727, and was knighted in 1746. Thomas Bootle died in 1753 and was buried at St Thomas's church, Melling. (*The Bootle Arms public house stands opposite the church*). A bachelor, he was succeeded initially by his brother and then by the latter's daughter, Mary, who married Richard Wilbraham of Rode Hall, Cheshire, in 1755. In accordance with the terms of the will of Sir Thomas, Richard assumed the surname of Bootle. However his son, Edward, born 1771, obtained a licence to take the additional surname of Wilbraham, and became Edward Wilbraham Bootle-Wilbraham. An MP from 1805-1828, he was created Baron

Skelmersdale in 1828. He died in 1853 and his estates passed to his grandson Edward Bootle-Wilbraham, who was created the first Earl of Lathom in 1880, Lathom House having been purchased by Thomas Bootle in 1724.

Earlier, in 1485, Lathom House had been visited by Henry VII, when it was the home of the Lathom family. They were granted the earldom of Derby after their Sir Thomas's services to Henry Tudor at the battle of Bosworth. (*A wing of the house still remains in Lathom Park.*) (Information: Ormskirk Civic Trust town centre exhibition, 17 February, 1990).
There is a Wilbraham Street near the Queensway Tunnel in Birkenhead, and another leads off Scotland Road, just before the slip-road to the Kingsway, Wallasey Tunnel. It was in this area that I last saw a woman whom I believed to be a 'Mary-Ellen', a typical Liverpool woman of that area, she being dressed in a long black skirt with a grey shawl around her shoulders. Her long hair was fastened back in a bun).

In the 1940's Mr and Mrs Case and their family of young men and women lived in Wilbraham Cottage. Thelma, a teenage daughter, was a particular friend of our family. She once made me a black tunic out of blackout material, set off by a red ribbon as a sash. This was the costume I wore when I tapdanced with 2 friends, Dorothy Critchley and Lilian Bond, on a concert, first performed at the Hut in Mount Road and then repeated on the hostels' stage. We danced to the song "Chewing a Piece of Straw". Our teacher was Miss Tina Weaver, a talented, pretty, petite lady, who held classes in ballet and tap on the top floor of her parents' home and shop at Melling Mount (*the site of Mount Garage*).

A few hundred yards further along Prescot Road, on the right-hand side, was Clarke's Farm where the elderly Prescot sisters lived. They, like many other local people, particularly enjoyed going to Ormskirk, the town famous for its tower and steeple church, its gingerbread, and its outdoor market. A single-decked Ribble bus, serviced the route between Liverpool and Ormskirk via Melling at sparse but regular intervals, and the driver, accompanied by a conductor, would conveniently stop at the top of the road, at the junction of Waddicar Lane and Prescot Road.

When the Misses Prescot left, Mr and Mrs Bill Mercer came to live in the stone-built house with their son and daughter, Bill and Matty. There was a small front garden, a cobbled yard, which Mrs Mercer used to weed regularly, outbuildings, a stable and a barn, and they had a duck pond which was set back a little from the road, on the Glover's Brow side of the property.

I was once delighted some years later at home when one of our ducks came out from a nettle patch followed closely by her newly hatched ducklings, walking in a line behind her. They waddled along as fast as their tiny webbed feet would let them, hopping over obstacles as they hurried to catch up with their proud mother. She watched me closely but trustingly, no loud quacking or flapping of wings, as, in order to help them towards smoother ground, I picked them up gently and placed them one by one in my apron. The eggs they produced when grown helped to make mother's custard pies extra tasty. (Cases' and Mercers' properties have now been demolished, the former having first been vandalised during the 1960s).

Pastoral scene

Chapter XII

☆ ☆ ☆

At home

My mother was rarely out when we arrived home from school but if she were we would usually sit and wait for her at the front of our house, on the small, sandstone wall, behind which stood tall poplar trees. (*The wall is lower now because the present footpath was made in front of it.*)

On the other hand, we might instead go into the dairy to help our father, either by rinsing and sorting the milk bottles

Mr Rigby who planted the Poplars circa 1914

— those bearing our own name from the 'foreigners', the latter being collected in at regular intervals — or go into the other room at the back of the dairy to top the pints of milk being filled by a hand-operated machine, Donald proving a speedy operator.

The bottles had wide necks. A cardboard top with a perforated hole in the middle was hand pressed to seal the bottle. Sometimes I made a simple brooch out of a top, by wrapping strands of wool in and out of the hole. The tops were packed in long cartons, about 2 feet (0.6096 metres) long, and an empty carton easily became a "telescope" in our childish imagination. Outside in the yard we often played leapfrog over the empty milk tanks, or cricket — if the ball went over the wire netting fencing around the hen run, extra runs were easily scored.

More daringly, we sometimes climbed up the ladder to the loft over the dairy (*later converted into an office*), or climbed the pear and apple trees, or attached a rope to a branch and swung from it like Tarzan.

Albert, Donald and me playing cricket

In springtime the garden smelt sweet with the scent of the pink and white apple blossom and the all-white pear blossom, which looked like summer snow. Our 3 apple trees all produced baking apples, of different varieties. One pear tree was high and produced small, soft, sweet pears with a yellowish-greenish skin, whereas the other tree nearer the house was shorter and produced at a later date a small, hard pear, not quite as sweet-tasting, with a reddish, russet-coloured skin. At the bottom of this tree there was a medium-sized sandstone trough.

In late summer, we often jumped over, and fell onto — much to the farm workers' annoyance — the freshly made hay stacks in the back fields, our limbs tanned shiny, golden brown by the sun.

In autumn Dad used to dig a 'spud' hole, that is, a potato hole in the back garden. This was a long trench which he filled with potatoes, these then being covered with straw before the soil was replaced on top in the shape of a sloping 'roof'.

When mother came home she usually made us chips for tea, or we would enjoy the delicious soup which she had earlier prepared. Food was kept in the pantry in a safe, which was a small standing cupboard with a wire-mesh door to keep out the flies in summer whilst at the same time letting in the air to keep the food fresh.

If I had been allowed to have my own way, I would have had toast for every meal! I made it at the coal fire, holding a round of bread at the end of a long toasting fork. Of course butter was a rare luxury, margarine being commonly used. However, when Donald and Albert went to Anglesey in North Wales to stay with Arthur Owen and his parents — Donald, always quick to make a friend, had met Arthur, of a similar age, when both were in Fazakerley hospital, where the latter had had his leg amputated — Mrs Owen sent mother a pat of home-made butter, with a stamp on the top. Rather salty in taste, all the family agreed that it was absolutely delicious (no butter since has ever tasted as good to us).

'Black' bread — rather more grey than black — was not welcome to our British taste, but was sometimes another wartime necessity. Mother supplemented our wartime diet with vitamin products, such as, rosehip syrup, orange juice, cod liver oil and malt, and a kind of blackcurrant purée.

Mother wrote regularly to her elder sister, Agnes, who had emigrated to Canada in the 1920s, sailing from Liverpool. She and her husband and 5 children lived in the prairie town of Winnipeg where they experienced very severe winters.

The eldest child, Beth, and the youngest, Tommy, were fit and healthy, but tragically the 3 middle sons, all suffered from muscular dystrophy and died when young — Bill living the longest — until he was 19 years old. He wrote a letter to me, which included a joke. Aunt Agnes once wrote to Dr Ainsworth to seek his help regarding a possible cure but it was hopeless. She tried diagnosing the cause herself, the only difference she could discover in the upbringing of her children was that these 3 boys had been inoculated by a different doctor. Around the age of 7 she noticed that her boys were easily blown over by the wind, and that the other children laughed at them. Despite everything, aunt Agnes never complained, once writing to my mother saying that she could always look out of the window and see someone else worse off than herself — my mother doubted that very much.

We children thought it very exciting to have Canadian relations. Our aunt sent us comics in which we read about such characters as the detective Dick Tracey, Superman, and Little Orphan Annie. For mother she sent a newspaper and its romantic novel supplement. From time to time we received a food parcel, in which she packed home-made shortbread — her husband, Bob, a Scottish emigrant, was a master baker — and sweets called 'lifesavers', which were like a polo mint but were more fruity in taste. Sometimes

Aunt Agnes, Uncle Bob and family in Canada

garments were included, like socks, scarves, gloves — she was an excellent knitter, and, like my mother, good at crochet work. (Years later aunt Agnes visited us during the 1950's, her first visit 'home' in 30 years.) We collected the Canadian stamps, adding them to our individual stamp collections, which were also increased by the addition of the stamps we selected to buy from the packets we received "on approval".

I also looked forward to the postman or postwoman bringing me news from the "Ovaltineys" club, on the wireless which

had a secret password (*which I still will not divulge!*) and its own signature tune — "We are the Ovaltineys little boys and girls. . . "

As a fervent film-fan, I often sent away for autographed photographs of famous film stars, like the English film star Margaret Lockwood. She starred in a thriller involving Germans, the action taking place on a European train. It was called "The Lady Vanishes". It was in black and white as were most films in those days. I saw it at the hostels.

Used envelopes were not thrown away because paper was rationed. The *"Daily Express"* went down to 4 pages but Lord Beaverbrook, the owner, ordered that Rupert Bear be preserved as being good for morale. We saved all kinds of paper and took it to school where it was collected and sent away for recycling. There was no litter problem then. Nothing was wasted. Coloured pieces of rag were used to make fireside peg rugs, a sack being used for the backing, and mother used to make rough aprons out of meal sacks. Cinders from the fire were sieved, the best of them then being mixed with slack and sometimes potato peelings to back up the fire.

Chapter XIII

Cause — Concentration Camp
Some major wartime events — Victory

Neville Chamberlain had been the British Prime Minister at the outbreak of the war. He had previously long sought to reach agreements with Germany and Italy and to preserve peace. On 31 March 1939 an Anglo-French agreement guaranteed aid to Poland in the event of aggression, this being expanded on 6 April into a mutual pact of assistance "in the event of any threat, direct, or indirect, to the independence of either". Germany attacked Poland on 1 September, with forces estimated at 1,700,000 men.

The Nazi party had been declared the only political party in Germany on 14 July 1933, and was noted for its ruthless persecution of the Jews. The Nuremberg Laws, established on 15 September 1935, deprived the Jews, including those of ¼ Jewish extraction, of citizenship, and all intermarriage with Jews was strictly forbidden.

During the war concentration camps were set up, the most notorious being Auschwitz, near Cracaw in Poland, it having 4 gas chambers, in which men, women, and children were slain. There are accounts elsewhere, of the horrors of the concentration camps, some of which — Belsen was on the cinema newsreels and in newspaper reports — we children witnessed, read about, could not believe, and wept over: "Man's inhumanity to man makes countless thousands mourn", Robert Burns, Scottish poet, 1786. When one thinks, these male and female camp commandants, who had committed such evil acts against men, women, and children, had once been children themselves. Perhaps if then, in childhood, they had taken responsibility for their future actions, committed themselves to try and always do good, thousands could have been spared intense suffering: "The Child is father of the Man", William Wordsworth, English poet, 1807

When labour shortage in Germany became scarce during the war, hundreds of thousands of French, Belgian, and Dutch were rounded up and sent to work in German factories, often living under the most appalling conditions. By the end there were about 7 million foreign 'slaves' with Nazi masters.

Chamberlain had resigned on 10 May 1940 and been replaced by Winston Churchill, who headed a coalition cabinet which included Labourites and Conservatives, his Foreign Secretary, Anthony Eden, being appointed on 23 December. Churchill inspired the British nation to victory, not with power nor threats, but with words, emotive words from our native English language. The following speech was made in 1940 when we stood alone and everything seemed hopeless as Hermann Goering, chief of Hitler's Luftwaffe — airforce — boasted that Britain would be annihilated but not one bomb would drop on Berlin:-

"Death and sorrow will be the companions of our journey; hardship our garment; constancy and valour our only shield. We must be united, we must be undaunted, we must be inflexible. Our qualities and deeds must burn and glow through the gloom of Europe until they become the veritable beacons of its salvation."

The Battle of Britain took place in 1940, the Luftwaffe opening an offensive designed to destroy British air strength. On 10 October London was heavily raided —

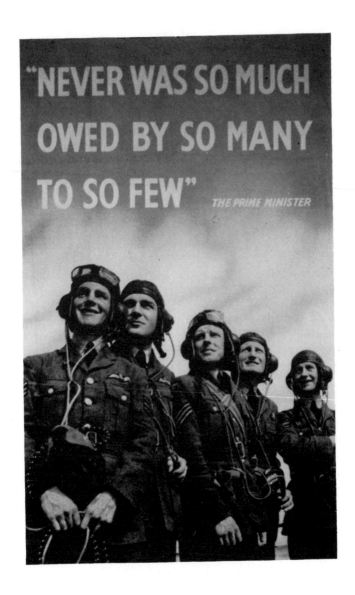

miraculously St Paul's cathedral survived. "The Battle of Britain was the first true air battle. It turned the tide of history by halting Hitler's advance and led ultimately to the Allied victory in Europe." quote from the Daily Express 15th September 1990.

To give the reader some idea of what could be involved in a dog fight the following report for the night of 12th March 1941, describes a battle in the air over Liverpool between a British Hurricane V7752, flown solo by Sergeant Robin McNair (now a Squadron Leader), and a German Heinkel 111 (a fighter bomber).

"McNair was at about 14,000 feet with the cockpit hood open for clearer visability and was very cold. After about fifteen minutes circling on station he saw a Heinkel 111 going south silhouetted against the cloud in the reflection from the searchlights. A steep turn brought him within range.

"He saw his bullets strike and leave their mark along the enemy's fuselage and wing. He banked away again to avoid the air gunners. There was no return fire, they must have been killed. But the Heinkel continued on its way.

"Sgt McNair came up behind and again attacked, but 25 yards is too close and he nearly collided. Oil from the Heinkel now covered his windscreen and he couldn't see anything, but as he broke away he could see the undercarriage of the bomber was hanging down and loose. The enemy had not yet dropped his bombs, and he must be prevented from doing so.

"The balloons by now were very near and, the fires from the city far below reflected red and angry on their undersides. Swerving he climbed steeply to avoid the cables. Acres of Liverpool and Birkenhead, as far as he could see to the horizon, were on fire. He knew he was not alone, the rest of the squadron was somewhere in the sky, but on such a night it was every man for himself until the leader called them back or the fuel ran out.

"The Heinkel dived suddenly and spiralled down, crashing into the Wirral, though McNair was too busy getting out of the way to note the detail."
(Extract quoted from "Fighter Pilot over Liverpool" Report by Eunice Wilson 247 Squadron Association's Archivist.)

On 10 November Coventry was blasted — this being a massive effort to crush British industrial resources and to demoralize the population. Britain had survived the worst of the blitz, but at a price, 14,000 civilians having been killed in London alone. William Langer, Coolidge Professor of History, Emeritus, Harvard University, records that "Enormous damage had been endured by the British with remarkable courage. One home in every five was damaged or destroyed, factories shattered, and transport, gas, and water systems disrupted."

On March 26, 1944, Churchill proclaimed:
"Britain. . . has never flinched or failed. And when the signal is given, the whole circle of avenging nations will hurl themselves upon the foe and batter out the life of the cruellest tyranny which has ever sought to bar the progress of mankind."

During 1944 on 6 June the allies landed in Normandy. In the same month came the defeat of the Japanese invasion of India. On 3 September Brussels was liberated. On 20 October the Americans landed in the Phillipines.

In 1945 on 23 March the British crossed the Rhine. On 2 May the German forces in Italy surrendered. On 5 May all the German forces in Holland, NW Germany and Denmark surrendered unconditionally. 8th May: VE Day — Victory celebrated — street parties. On 9 May the unconditional surrender of Germany to the Allies was ratified in Berlin. On 10 June the Australian troops landed in Borneo.

On 6 August the first atomic bomb dropped on Hiroshima.

On 8 August Russia declared war on Japan.

On 9 August the second atomic bomb dropped on Nagazaki. On 14 August the Emperor of Japan broadcast the unconditional surrender of his country. 15th August — VJ (Victory over Japan) Day.

The trial of major Nazi leaders opened at Nuremberg on 20 November 1945. On 30 September 1946 the International Tribunal announced its decision, the boastful Hermann Goering avoiding execution by committing suicide.

Bill and Len had not died in vain, goodness had triumphed over evil and peace had been restored. The aggressors — Germany under its Fuhrer, Adolf Hitler, who committed suicide in Berlin on 20 April 1945, — and Japan, led by the Emperor Hirohito who continued to rule Japan until his death in 1989 — had been overthrown. The British Commonwealth celebrated victory along with its allies — Russia led by their communist leader, Generalissimo Joseph V. Stalin; America by President Franklyn Roosevelt, who, despite being in a wheelchair, had played a full part in defeating the enemies of freedom; and China, by General Chiang Kai-Shek, a Chinese nationalist, whose wife, Madame Chiang Kai-Shek, shared the world stage with her husband. He had been a remarkable soldier in his youth, having defied Japan's invasion of his country during 1937-45.

At school on 8 June 1946 British schoolchildren received the following message from the King:-

"Today as we celebrate victory I send this personal message to you and all other boys and girls at school. For you have shared in the hardship and dangers of a total war and you have shared no less in the triumph of the allied nations. I know you will always feel proud to belong to a country which was capable of such supreme effort, proud too of parents and elder brothers and sisters who by their courage, endurance and enterprise brought victory. May these qualities be yours as you grow up and join in the common effort to establish among the nations of the world unity and peace. George R.I."

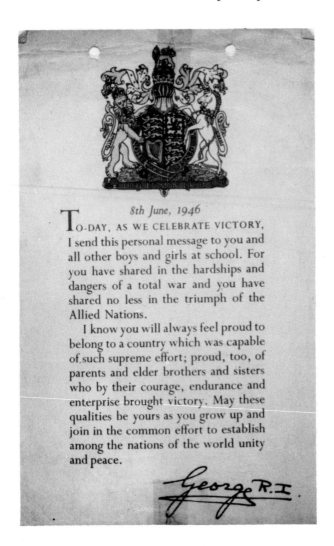

8th June, 1946

To-day, as we celebrate victory, I send this personal message to you and all other boys and girls at school. For you have shared in the hardships and dangers of a total war and you have shared no less in the triumph of the Allied Nations.

I know you will always feel proud to belong to a country which was capable of such supreme effort; proud, too, of parents and elder brothers and sisters who by their courage, endurance and enterprise brought victory. May these qualities be yours as you grow up and join in the common effort to establish among the nations of the world unity and peace.

George R.I.

(On the back of the message card there is a list of the main war dates — some of which I have aforementioned — and at the bottom are the words "MY FAMILY'S WAR RECORD").

Chapter XIV

Holiday in Scotland
Meeting a First World War Veteran
Poetry and Songs – Wilfred Owen
Breaking up of The Kirkby Wartime
Community.

That summer of 1946 I had the second of the 2 holidays I had so far spent with my parents — one before the war and one after it. They took Albert and me to Bearsden, a suburb of Glasgow, Scotland, by train from Exchange Station, in Tithebarn Street, Liverpool — Donald staying at home to look after the business. We stayed with Mr and Mrs John Izaat, who were friends of a Park Lane, Aintree, milk customer.

Like my parents, they too had a milk business, but they had a shop in Glasgow and did not have milk rounds. Instead they only undertook large orders, such as supplying the ships which frequented the port of Glasgow. A qualified chemist, Mrs Izaat told me that her father had bequeathed a large sum of money to her, but only on the understanding that she use it to travel as much as possible because he believed that to be the finest education one could have.

During our stay we visited Mr and Mrs Bobbie Parker. Mr Parker had been a footballer in his youth, once playing for

Mr Parker as a young footballer circa 1909

Everton. Dad's uncle Bill, an Everton director and later Chairman, had requested that we visit them, as he had known Bobbie when the latter played at Goodison Park. When we met him he was in a wheelchair, an invalid. As a soldier in the First World War — the war during which my mother as a child at Melling school had joined her classmates in knitting garments for the war effort — he had been wounded by shrapnel and left paralysed. It was quite difficult to equate the handsome, wavy haired young footballer on a sepia-coloured photograph with the smiling weighty gentleman who, with his caring wife, greeted us with such warmth. He kept a rota of names to mention in his nightly prayers. During the war this had included men and women in the allied forces. He told us, saddened at the thought, that one night he had forgotten one young serviceman's name and the latter had been killed.

A gifted artist, he gave my mother 2 wax-like wall plaques which he had made, one depicting birds in flight and the other garden flowers. Mr Parker obtained the material from France. (Perhaps he, in fact, practised Découpage — a craft whereby, not wax, but actually cardboard is doubled up and varnished several times with a very fine brush.) Mr Parker also gave us a very special gift, a book in which he had written down poems, some of which he had copied, and others which he himself had composed whilst fighting in the cold, rat infested muddy trenches during the French campaigns of World War I, 1914-18.

The late A J P Taylor FBA in his book "English History 1914-1945" commented that ". . . the second world war, unlike the first, produced no distinctive literature. There were no war poets during the war. . . . Some young men who were already poets continued to write poetry when they were in the services. This did not make them war poets in the sense that Blunden, Sassoon, or Owen had been. . . ." He described Wilfred Owen, 1893-1918, as ". . . incomparably the greatest poet of either war,. . . ."

Born at Oswestry in Shropshire, Owen attended Birkenhead Institute during the time his father, Tom Owen, held a supervisory post at Birkenhead with the Great Western and London and North Eastern Railways, living in turn at 14 Willmer Road, 7 Elm Grove, and 51 Milton Street, 1897-1899. Owen has been described as being sensitive, shy, and outstandingly brave in action. He focused his writing on 'the pity of war', and produced poems "of unparalleled poignancy and compassion". He regarded himself as a 'Georgian' poet, the poetry of plain language, sharpness of detail, and a commitment to realism that did not avoid the unpleasant.

Although of a pacifist inclination, he felt impelled to enlist in October 1915. During part of his training he stayed at 168a Lord Street, Southport, October 1916. Owen returned to France after a period of repatriation owing to his being shell-shocked. When mentioning the Red Cross Hospital at Maghull in his book "Lydiate & Maghull in Times Past" John K. Rowlands states "... and the first 20 shell-shocked patients were admitted on December 4th 1914. Major Richard Rows brought together an outstanding team of workers which included Dr. Rivers who treated the war poets Siegfried Sassoon and Wilfred Owen." The young poet soldier fell leading his men across the Sambre Canal on 4 November 1918. The Armistice was signed on 11 November 1918.

My mother's uncle, Henry Mattocks, was killed in that war. He was 21 years of age. Her 2 older brothers also served in the First World War — Eben, who was mustard gassed and suffered as a result for the rest of his life, and Jim, who was in the army of occupation in Germany. He spoke well of the local Germans. The songs they, Mr Parker, and their comrades sung, which were carried over to World War II, included "Pack up your troubles in your old kit-bag and smile, smile, smile. . . " and the song given to that war by Ireland — "It's a long way to Tipperary, it's a long way to go. . . " the song sung during the first world war by the great numbers of Irishmen who volunteered for the British army. Over 200,000 of them joined up and 60,000 never returned. As Sean O'Casey, the famous Irish playwright in Irish tragedy, described the scene in Dublin, watching thousands singing that song as they marched to the troopships: "The stoutest men from hill, valley and town came pressing into the British army. Long columns of Irishmen went swinging past Liberty Hall down to the quays, to the ships waiting to take them to a poppy-mobbed grave in Flanders." During the second world war Southern Ireland like several other countries, for example, Switzerland, remained neutral.

World War II had ended and my primary schooldays which had started with it, had also ended. New experiences lay ahead, and new pleasures — making new friends like May Tither from Billinge near Wigan, learning French, how to play hockey, and rushing home from school to listen to the nightly Dick Barton radio series, which was to be introduced in the autumn of 1946. I had passed the scholarship and gained entry to Upholland Grammar School, near Wigan (a town to which I am still devoted because of the friendliness, modesty, and outstanding quality of treating other people with respect which is practised by its inhabitants. I am honoured to be a vice president of Wigan Ladies Hockey Club, having played for them in my youth.)

The breaking up of the classroom group at Kirkby school was reflected on a wider scale by the breaking up of the wartime-formed Kirkby community. The Americans — some now with English wives, referred to as GI brides — returned home. Later, a friend, Joan Brown, told me of her parents' plans to leave 10 Sefton Close and emigrate to London, Ontario, Canada, by ship from Southampton, to join their relatives (we still correspond, and Joan has been back several times). I longed to go too, and planned to save my pocket money until I had sufficient for the fare! However, not all the people who had come to live in Kirkby left — many of the southerners stayed on, for example, Mr and Mrs Powell and their children in Mount Road, and Mr and Mrs Simmons and their daughter, Pat, in North Park Road.

Today it is probably difficult for Joan and others returning to Kirkby, or for someone visiting it for the first time, to visualise some of the scenes I have described because they are now simply derelict patches of land, overgrown with weeds, — the sites of the hostels, the railway cottages, the school, Atherton's cottage/sweet shop, and the waterworks. The lovely house at Mill Farm, Wilbraham Cottage, and Clarke's farmhouse and outbuildings are gone but, in my heart, they are all, as Arthur Mee described the churchyard in the 1930s, ". . . as trim as a garden". They are as vibrant as they were 50 years ago when I took my first walk to school in the village of Kirkby.

Postscript

Today I have German friends, Elvira and her husband Manfred. They call me "schwester" — German for "sister". Their kindness and hospitality are exceptional.

I drive a car which has a Japanese engine, because our country has trade agreements with Japan.

This year the football World Cup '90 took place in Italy — land of our wartime enemy — and thousands of British fans flocked there and savoured the delights of the scenery and sunny climate of that beautiful country, and cities of culture, like the world famous magnificent city of Florence, as well as enjoyed the matches between the various countries, several of whom had been wartime enemies.

My story, I believe, reveals that one does not forget the people and experiences of childhood; that wars bring great sorrow — life can be difficult enough anyway; and that loving relationships give one the greatest happiness, comfort, and support.

Therefore my hope for the children of today, for the individual's happiness, is best expressed in those words of King George VI, that

". . . you grow up and join in the common effort to establish among the nations of the world unity and peace."

Epilogue

WILLIAM DONALD BIRCH
29.12.28 — 30.6.87

Donald was blessed with a happy marriage to Pauline, daughter of the late Mr and Mrs Duffy of Mickering Lane, Aughton. She was his constant inspiration and support throughout his illness, unfailing in her devotion. He was very proud of her.

A loving father to Dianne, Philip and Susan, he was much loved in return, and was happy when Dianne married Hobeddine from Tunisia, welcoming him into the family. A few years later Pauline and Donald became grandparents, first of all a grand-daughter, Chantal, and later a grandson, Matthew. Some years earlier I had asked Donald why Pauline and he were keeping the swing in their garden as their children had grown up. He had replied,"Well, we hope to have grandchildren one day," his whole attitude being that of a family man.

Mother says of her caring and dutiful son, "He was loved when he came into the world and he was loved when he went out." Our father cherishes **all** memory of him, but now and again he will divulge a particular father-son memory, thereby expressing the depth of feeling which only that special relationship can bring. The other day he spoke of the time when Donald was about 4 years old and he bought him

Donald and Pauline

small hedge shears from George Weir who supplied farm and garden equipment. As his small boy stood alongside him by the hedge, copying his father's skill, an old farm labourer, Abram Kidd, whom Dad much admired and respected for his farming and countryside knowledge, went past and commented, " He'll be an expert when he gets older!'' A simple event but it still makes Dad very happy — and proud — to recall it. (And it is true that Donald always did trim a hedge well).

For Albert, Ann and me, we greatly miss a protective older brother who was always willing to defend us, listen to, and try to understand our problems, and then to advise.

In manhood Donald, who, like Albert became a director in the family dairy business, was approximately 5 feet 9 inches

*Our parents' Golden Wedding celebration at The Prince of Wales Hotel
Southport 1978*

(approximately. 1.75 metres) in height, and weighed around
11 stone (approximately. 154lbs or 70 kilos). Although his
hair was black he had inherited the Celtic colouring of his
maternal grandparents — his skin being fair, his cheeks
glowing red in the wintertime.

Girls sought his company, but he had once had the
'brush-off' — when he was 7 years old! Then living in
Netherton, he was informed by a childhood sweetheart,
Dora Houghton, that she had another boyfriend: "That's all
right", replied Donald, in his usual optimistic way, "you've
got 2 now".

Of an outgoing personality, he loved company and was
loved by it in return, always being made welcome at
neighbours' houses, and in turn always making visitors
welcome. Donald enjoyed a good joke, whilst at the same
time deploring anything in bad taste that could offend or

Dad and Donald in Netherton in the early thirties

hurt anyone. He was a born entertainer and could easily make people laugh — once he and a friend from the youth club, Ernie Perry, were spotted by a theatre talent scout when performing a double act on a concert, but they never took up the offer.

His hazel eyes often twinkled with good humour and affection — he smiled with his eyes. Sometimes they grew sad with despair, and, very occasionally, they flashed with anger. He had the gift of understanding people, and was always willing to listen to one's problems, offering sympathy when necessary. He had *TIME* for everyone, a rare quality. No words, however, can adequately describe, do justice to, the warmth of his presence.

For his 'likes' he was an occasional cigarette smoker, an intermittent social drinker; food — he enjoyed a bacon and 2-egg breakfast, and chips for everything else! Other favourites were homemade cakes and pies — if I asked him if he wanted a piece of pie, even if he was on his way out, he would initially say, "No thanks, 'I' ", only to follow it up with, "Oh, well, I don't mind". His voice was well-modulated, not gruff or harsh at all.

An idiosyncrasy of Don's was, when leaving, he would say "Cheerio, Dad," and to anyone else in the house as he went out of the door. One would wait a minute or two and then, sure enough, the door would open again and he would be back, having forgotten something!

His concern with cleanliness in all things was famous in the family, especially with his food product, milk. When we washed our own bottles they would have to be gleaming before he was satisfied. (Today milk is frequently sold in cartons, not making it as easy for the consumer to check the contents with the naked eye).

A perfectionist at all times, his handwriting was immaculate, as was his figure-work in accounting, the former being neat and written in a script-like style — a pleasure to look at — and the latter also being exact to the last penny. Perhaps he was **too** honest for a businessman! "As straight as a dye" Dad would say.

He was always well-groomed. "Just like his Grandad Birch", Dad would comment as he watched Donald polishing his shoes — even on rainy days — with the same determination and desire for perfection as a silversmith has before putting his goods on display in his shop. Brylcreem hair cream, sports jacket and flannels, were the fashionable social dress of his youth, ties coming in abundance as birthday and Christmas gifts.

Donald had great charisma. However, when someone, or something, displeased him very much he would either give the person a "look" of contempt, or simply express it as if to himself, apparently always confident enough in his own judgement of a person or a situation.

Like Dad, whilst in agreement with, and being a great admirer of, standards, he was critical of any form of snobbery, materially or intellectually based. He deplored hypocrisy, thereby copying his parents' Christian outlook. No tramp, such as Billy, was ever turned away from our door. Billy would be given a mug of tea and sandwiches. Then off he would go towards Ormskirk and Preston. "Some rich widows live in Ormskirk" he would say to my mother. He had a long beard but his eyes made one think he was actually younger than he at first appeared, because they were such a piercing blue.

As regards his Christian faith, Donald was devout, yet never flamboyant or flaunting in his religious beliefs. In his illness he drew great comfort from those beliefs. Our last day's outing was to Stonyhurst College, Hurst Green, near Preston. He was very impressed with the chapel there, particularly interested in the stations of the cross carved in wood.

Any boy who had the good fortune to work alongside Donald had one of the greatest teachers of all time — many proving it by going on to be successful in life, with careers in the police, in banks, or by setting up in business. To be around someone who is a constant example of the correct moral way to behave in one's approach to people, to life in general, is to have the best teacher in the world, the finest education.

Like his father, he was an Everton shareholder, both being keen Evertonians. Dad used to enjoy spotting potential players, his hero from youth being the Everton idol Dixie Dean. Dad's uncle Bill — William Richard Williams — became Chairman of Everton during the 1950s, the days of players like Farrell, Eglington, T. G. Jones, Wainwright, Sagar, Grant, and Stevenson. Uncle Bill had a quiet but determined disposition. He was a self-made Liverpool businessman, a coal merchant with premises in Cherry Lane, Walton.

Dad's Uncle Bill chatting with Everton players when he was Chairman

Everton Football Club. Dad's Uncle Bill second from left

Uncle Bill's manager in the doorway of his office in Walton

Donald's funeral service was held at St Michael's Church, Aughton, where he had married Pauline, and where he had but a few years earlier given their daughter, Dianne, away in marriage. The church was full to overflowing, with relatives, friends from the masonic lodge, Ceres, in which he had held high rank, including that of Worshipful Master, nuns from the local Kirkby convent in North Park Road, Liverpool football supporters and Evertonians, all united in their love and respect for Donald.

As one of his friends who read the sermon said, "Although it is a very sad occasion, the church is also full of happiness, Donald being remembered for the laughter he brought into people's lives." Even in his last illness, when he had to wear a metal halo-like vice which was fitted onto his shoulders and screwed into his temples in order to support his neck, he laughed when an old miner from Wigan in Wrightington hospital remarked: "A man from outer space, my family won't believe me!", and he put Sister Emmanuel at ease by saying: "You didn't think I'd get my halo before you!" because he knew people were a little horrified when they first saw the halo.

Donald never lost his fighting spirit, first shown as a 13-year-old boy in hospital — still burning in the 58-year-old man — saying "We'll win yet, Dad", as he took his mother in his arms. That night driving home to Kirkby, my parents commented on the beautiful sky, with a magnificent rainbow over Aughton, "as if Heaven were opening its doors to the world", little realising that Donald was dying — he had kept that from them to the end. Next morning my mother heard the song "Somewhere over the Rainbow" — the song made famous by the late Judy Garland — played on the radio — it was one of Donald's favourite songs.

At the funeral, outside the church, Gert Bradley (née Newsholme) looked around at the men making hay in the field beside the church on that summer's day and said "Don Birch!", thus summing up that he was sunshine, peace, and a part of the English countryside, like the picture he had bought our mother — her favourite — Constable's "The Haywain". Another testimony was expressed by his former neighbour, Mr Twiss, who, though crippled, walked back to St Michael's having been put off the bus at Christ Church by mistake. He said, "I would have climbed Everest for Don!"

Donald was a proud man but there was no vanity, and he retained his dignity to the end of his life, being described by his many grieving friends as "a gentleman".

BIBLIOGRAPHY

The Windsor Story, J. Bryan and Charles J. V. Murphy (Granada Publishing Ltd 1981).
Walking Tall, Simon Weston (Bloomsbury Publishing Ltd 1989).
Pears Almanack.
The Second World War Vol. VI (Triumph and Tragedy), Winston S. Churchill (Cassell & Co Ltd 1954).
Traditions, Superstitions & Folklore, Charles Hardwick (E. J. Morten 1872).
Chronicle of 20th Century, Longman Chronicle Communications, Lond. (Conceived and Published by Jacques Legrand SA Paris for the Chronicle-System, Harenberg Kommunication, Dortmund 1988).
Discovering Women's History (A Practical Manual), Deirdre Beddoe (Pandora Press 1983).
Cyclopaedia of Initials and Abbreviations, F. Dubrez Fawcett (London Business Publications 1963).
Cassells Dictionary of Initials, comp. by J. W. Gurnett and C. H. J. Kyte (Cassell & Co 1972).
Conflict in the 20th Century, Charles Messenger, Ed. Dr. J. Pimlott.
The Kirkby Font, Charles F. Larkin 1919 (Kirkby Library Ref. 729.91).
The Kings England LANCASHIRE, Arthur Mee (Hodder & Stoughton 1936).
Good Housekeeping Magazine, October 1989.
The Milk Industry Magazine, July 1930.
Liverpool Echo, 12 February 1990.
A Short History of Lathom, Peter Smith (Pilkington Bros. PLC Printing Dept. 1981).
Daily Express, 17 August 1989.

Encyclopaedia of World History, comp. & ed. by William A. Langer (George C. Harrap & Co Ltd 1940-1968).

Chronology of World War II (Day by Day Illustrated Record 1939-1945), compiled by Christopher Argyle.

Britain Under Fire (Bombing of Britain's Cities), Charles Whiting (Century Hutchings Ltd 1986).

The Fifth Year of War in Pictures, Odhams Press Ltd.

English History 1914-1945, J. P. Taylor FBA (Oxford University Press 1965).

The Poems of Wilfred Owen, Edited by John Stallworthy (Hogarth Press, London 1988).

Great Poets, Geoffrey Chaucer, William Shakespeare, The Romantic Poets, The War Poets, (Marshall Cavendish Ltd MCMLXXXIX).

Great War – An Anthology, Ed. by Dominic Ibberd & John Onions (Macmillan Publishers Ltd 1986).

IRELAND, An Illustrated History, John Ranelagh (Collins 1981).

Human Documents of the Lloyd George Era, E. Royston Pike (Unwin University Books, George Allen & Unwin Ltd 1972).

Official Guide and Review, Kirkby Urban District Council (Home Publishing Co Ltd Surrey).

Kirkby 1066-1966 (Leaflet), Kirkby Local History Society.

Ordnance Survey Map, Lancashire sheet XCIX N.E. Revision of 1925 with additions in 1938

The History of Kirkby, by A.G. Plant, 1988. John Evans Design & Print, Southport.

Lydiate & Maghull in Times Past, John K. Rowlands, 1986, Published by Countryside Publications Limited, Chorley, Lancs

Beautiful Huyton with Roby: A Charming Residential Suburb — Andrew G. Colwell, 1980

"Fighter Pilot over Liverpool" Report by Eunice Wilson, 247 Squadron Archivist

"Daily Express" 15 September 1990

Ormskirk Civic Trust Town Cemntre Exhibition 17 February 1990

Acknowledgments

Relatives

Mr. A. L. Birch
Mrs. P. A. Birch
Mr. and Mrs. W. Birch
Mrs. J. Green
Mrs. E. Neilson
Mrs. A. Tyrer

Friends

Mrs. P. Abraham
Miss M. Ainsworth
Miss S. Atherton

Mr. P. Bretherton
Mr. J. Bullen
Mr. J. R. Bullen
Mrs. M. Cheetham
Mrs A. Dodd
Mr. D. Duffey
Mrs. Hill
Mrs. J. Johnson
Mr. A. Matthews
Mrs N. Parkinson
Mrs A. Wharton
Mrs B. Whittle
Mr. J. Woods

'Academic'

BBC Archives
Miss Andrea Ellis, *Heritage Officer*, Mrs Irene Vickers and
Mr E. E. Jackson, Croxteth Hall, Liverpool
Mr. K. Hall, *County Archivist*, Preston
Imperial War Museum, London
Mr. F. Kelly, *Ex-employee*, British Enka
Ian Hilder, B.A. (Hons), *Genealogical and Photographic Services*
Huyton Library

Knowsley Borough Council Staff and Southdene Estate
Offices
Knowsley Library Service
Ormskirk Library Staff
Ovaltine Organization
Picton Library Staff, Liverpool
Mr. N. Smith, *Senior Assistant*, Reference Library, Kirkby
Branch Library
Mr. Steve Young, *Information Assistant*, London Midland
British Rail Public Affairs, Birmingham
Fighter Pilot Over Liverpool, Report by Eunice Wilson, 247
Squadron Archivist. Daily Express, 15 September, 1990.
Ormskirk Civic Trust Town Centre Exhibition, 17 February,
1990.
Ordnance Survey Maps/OS 100NW, 1938.
Wirral Metropolitan College Library Staff

Special Mention

Mr. T. Charnley, *Lecturer*, Wirral Metropolitan College, who
collated my various notes and without whom this book
would not have been completed.
Mr. T. Morley, *Managing Director*, Print Origination (NW)
Ltd., whose enthusiasm for, and confidence in, my book
inspired me to continue.

BIOGRAPHY

Irene Birch's parents, William and Bethia Birch came to live at Alick's House Farm, Glover's Brow, Kirkby, in 1936, when she was 15 months old. They still live there, taking an active part in the family dairy business.

Miss Birch, B.Ed (Hons), was a lecturer in Business Technology at Wirral Metropolitan College, Birkenhead, having previously taught in a girls' finishing school, 'Montesano', in Gstaad, Switzerland. Trained at Garnett College (London University affiliated) she initially taught at Oxford College of Technology, returning home to teach at Ruffwood Comprehensive School, where she became Head of the Office Arts department and Careers Mistress, particularly enjoying her 3 years as a class tutor to the same group of pupils.

Her account of the history of Wirral Metropolitan College, undertaken as an assignment during preparation for her degree at Bolton College of Education (Manchester University affiliated) 1979, is in constant demand in the reference section of the college library.

It was the aim in both accounts to try to emphasise the personal experience, contribution, when staged against the backcloth of the public events which make history.